ROWING HOME

A 58-Year-Old Woman's
Record-Breaking Odyssey
Across the Atlantic

Suzanne Pinto

WINTER ISLAND PRESS

ISBN: 979-8-9925945-4-6
LCCN: 2025919589
First edition 2025

Published by Winter Island Press
3 Winter Island Road
Salem, Massachusetts 01970
www.winterislandpress.com
winterislandpress@gmail.com

Winter Island Press is dedicated to publishing books that reflect the breadth and bounty of the human experience.

Cover by Klassic Designs

To my family, Boulder Community Rowing,
and the Gloucester Gig Rowers,
for your support and inspiration
and for believing in adventure.

"I chose to fly the Atlantic because I wanted to.
It was, in a measure, a self-justification - a proving to me that
a woman with adequate experience could do it."

Amelia Earhart, The Fun of It

GOING TO EXTREMES: OLDER ADULTS ARE TESTING THEIR LIMITS WITH EXTREME SPORTS

Nicole Lehpamer, March 21, 2020

Now more than ever, older adults are testing their physical limits by engaging in sports more commonly practiced by young people, such as surfing, skiing, whitewater rafting, skateboarding, and even running marathons. In the past decade, for instance, the number of those aged 60 and better who register for the Ironman (a 140.6-mile and 70.3-mile triathlon) has quintupled from about 2,500 participants in 2012 to nearly 13,000 in 2022. Likewise, while the average Iditarod (a multiday, multi-method race through subzero Alaskan temperatures) participant in the 1900s was in their 30s, the average participant age is now 46.

Older adults now have time to accomplish many of the goals they had set in their youth and are more inclined to reach them. They find that pursuing goals helps prevent boredom and sedentary habits that sometimes become more routine with age.

Older women have particularly taken advantage of opportunities to test their physical limits, because they weren't given the same opportunities to engage in such enduring activities as their male counterparts in the past. While laws prior to the 1970s prohibited women from engaging in activities like marathons, the enactment of Title IX (prohibiting sex-based discrimination in federally funded schools) has given women the opportunity to engage in male-dominated sports. With this law also came a cultural shift in how women are perceived in sports. For instance, a 67-year-old female surfer noted that, while men never took her seriously as a female surfer in the past by claiming the best waves, they are now far less territorial. Moreover, all women now grow up being able to conceive of themselves as doing sports and keeping fit.

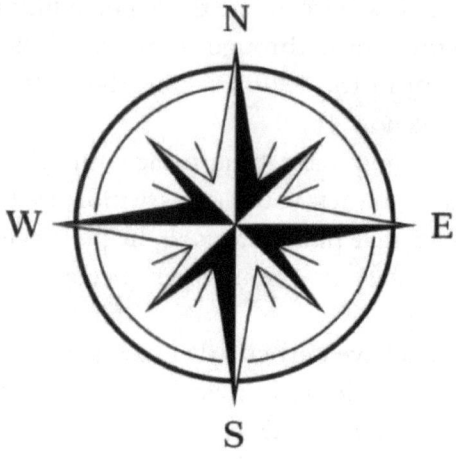

Prologue

Grim terror etches the faces of the crew. Even the youngest looks broken as wall after wall of water pummel the *Britannia III*. With each thirty-five-foot wave, someone is knocked out of their shoes and off their seat, thrown across the rigging or smashed up against the bow cabin wall. Only tenacity and Thor's grip keep us from being tossed overboard and lost in the rapacious flint grey sea. Darkness engulfs us. We are soaked and afraid.

Pain assaults every fiber of my body. My hips are screaming. The delts I've been so carefully curating for months are spasming like lightning in a hurricane and my hands are pulp. Our rear ends are already bubbling with bloody "diaper" rash. I intermittently row one-handed, supporting myself off my burning buttocks with the other hand, hoping for some relief from the constant salty friction of the seat. The two rowing gel seats and two sheepskin pads make no difference at all.

The oars become truncheons, clenched more like weapons against the waves than tools for steering through them. They bash our shins and send shocks of pain through our legs. We are all covered with abrasions, and every cut and scrape is infected and inflamed. The three long rents in my left knee are pus-filled and aching.

Seasickness racks each of us in spite of every antidote we've tried: expensive Scopolamine patches, Dramamine, pressure bracelets. We were told this would happen. Not leaving anything to chance, I used all three, and yet the vomiting is incessant. From where I sit, in the stroke seat at the stern, just looking at the GPS meter convulses my stomach. Captain Simon passes out cans of peaches. Stroke, vomit, stroke, stroke, vomit.

✦

Just three days earlier, on January 31, 2011, a sundry crew of fourteen ambitious rowers, four women and ten men, set off from Puerto de Mogán, in the Canary Islands, in a crazy bullet of a rowboat in search of Barbados and a couple of world records. I was the oldest person on board and the oldest woman ever to row across the Atlantic, so at least one of those records would be mine.

The trip was a year in the planning, and everything that could go wrong did. Weather, currents, power struggles—I mean, everything. And, as is so often the case, many of the problems had to do with personalities bashing up against each other like waves in a typhoon. But we were making it work. Sort of.

People tell me this is a story about grit and determination, persistence and compulsive positivity in the face of impending disaster, profound frustration, and slaphappy flying fish. To me, it's a tale of toughing it out, doing what you say you're going to do, following through. It's also about knowing who you are and being that person no matter what or who other people are telling you to be. And it's about them: beloved crew, bloody wankers. Human nature is bizarre.

Thanks to an interesting—okay, troublesome—childhood, I developed a talent early on for close observation and assessment of my fellow humans. This isn't always a blessing, of course, especially when you're living in very close quarters with a bunch of strangers. Never one to miss a chance to make lemonade, I took advantage of the hours—and hours, and hours—at sea to understand myself, my relationships, and my shipmates.

A psychologist by trade, this is something I'd been doing all my life, professionally and otherwise. What I hadn't done so much was to hold up a mirror. Weeks on the ocean, lightyears from land, sliding around in (you hope) your own bodily fluids and just waiting for it all to be over—it's impossible to avoid the introspection that I'd been successfully dodging for most of my adult life. Yet here we were.

✦

Rowing shift over, we crawl into our flooded "girls' cabin," too exhausted and cold to remove our foul weather gear. Our breath condenses overhead, then rains back down on us as we try to block out the pain, the howling wind, the lurching sway. Sleep is impossible. I am terrified. Anna and Jen lie huddled in life jackets, clasping hands and frantically praying, "…Holy Mary, mother of God, pray for us sinners, now and at the hour of our death…." Not wanting it to be the hour of my death, I whisper my own mantra: "Captain Simon knows what he's doing, the boat won't flip, we aren't going to die." But, under the onslaught, I start to wonder.

It is Day 3 of our thirty-three-day record-breaking endeavor to row across the Atlantic Ocean. Dear God, what have I gotten myself into? I just want to go home.

PART ONE

Before Before

1

How I Got Into This Mess

The origin of my exploits on the Atlantic started somewhat earlier. Maybe the seed was planted when Mike, my husband, moved to Liberia–yes, Africa–for three years. Or maybe it was before that, after my kids, my two favorite adventure buddies, grew up and flew away, leaving our mountain home in Boulder a little too quiet and me with a little too much time to think. Maybe I'd been ready to hit the high seas since my first marriage fell apart, or when I decided not to dwell in the drama of a tumultuous upbringing, or when I finally figured out I couldn't save everybody that needed saving.

My mother had been a nurse with a shatterproof creed: "No whining." A bright and curious Columbia University graduate, Midge had the interesting fortune to be born Roman Catholic at the cusp of women's sociological change. Capable women then still relinquished their careers to stay at home with too many children whom, at least in our case, their parents could ill afford to raise. Her life was further defined by the cancer that robbed her of a kidney and later dragged her through the slow and excruciating attrition of the rest of her body, pulverizing her bones and robbing her of herself until she died at the age of forty-two. I was fourteen when she first became sick, too young to understand/realize the enormity of her pain.

Midge created us in her image, to be strong, to swallow pain and forge ahead. She was an inordinately brave woman who herself never complained, neither about the pain nor being nursed through a two-years-long final excruciating illness by semi-resentful and wholly inept adolescent children. She never divulged her grief about abandoning her close-knit family up north to move to a foreign Puerto Rico, an ocean away from the community she had known her whole life. Nor did she complain, if she knew, about her philanderous husband, nor about his being the adored parent. She never uttered a peep about the bad hand she'd been dealt. A very bad hand.

I believe that my mother, a tiny beautiful woman with big dimples, the woman who danced and laughed at parties and with friends, found her worth in doing good deeds. We always had orphans over for Christmas and were required to give them one of our presents. She founded the League of Women Voters in San Juan, Puerto Rico, and shook governmental corruption by hands-on testing of the fetid water that saturated la Laguna de Condado. Her highly effective protests changed the laws about pumping waste from the hotels and establishments flanking La Laguna.

We were expected to operate at the same level, recognizing and calling out injustice in addition to volunteering. It was our duty to give back to our community. My mother was an honorable woman. It was her courage, strength, and motivation that may have propelled my adventure. And our relationship was deeply troubled.

My mother didn't seem to like her children. Our exuberance, passion, and laughter seemed to embarrass her. One evening, post "fancy dinner" at the landmark Swiss Chalet, an authentically built replica chalet moldering in the heat of the island, we kids burst out of the restaurant in high spirits, yes being very silly, our parents trailing us. It was a beautiful night, clear and warm and exotic. We linked arms, skipping and singing at the top of our lungs.

"When you're a Jet, you're a Jet all the way!" we laughed and danced.

"Stop that please," my mother hissed from behind. "You are embarrassing me." She looked like she was about to explode.

My Dad? I think he would have loved to link arms and skip down the street with us, skilled and stylish dancer that he was.

✢

After our mother's death, all five of us kids dispersed, believing we were sorely lacking in many respects. And all of us would, by God, overachieve to compensate.

My younger sister Carol, the most bitter and aggrieved of the siblings, emailed a few years ago.

"Hey," she wrote. "I cannot do it. I cannot think of anything nice about Mom."

Brother John from Seattle agreed. "Me neither, not much. But who cares?"

Debbie, the oldest, chimed in. "I care a lot that she hated me."

I couldn't help myself. My job had always been to understand.

"Hey," I wrote, wary but committed, "let's experiment

with engendering positive memories of Mom.''

We tried really hard. I remembered the time she marched me back to the Sister Superior, who had just suspended me because my too large breasts gaped the buttons of my 'girls' uniform shirt, and I was clearly enticing the boys. My mother sizzled the air in the room with her scolding.

"God gave my daughter ample breasts and who are you, Mother Superior, a servant of the Lord, to shame God's work?" Mother Superior wilted under Mom's protest and agreed I could purchase the boy's shirts as my uniform. So yes, she defended us.

She also expected perfection. She taught us always to do our best and to have excellent manners. In fact, Miss Manners was her bible. Debbie and I were enrolled in Miss Covington's school to learn ballroom dancing and proper etiquette.

But we felt we were never good enough. She criticized and admonished and shamed. Perhaps she wanted us to be what she could never be. She chastised us for being lazy and fat (although we were neither). She sent my sister Debbie and me to Weight Watchers at eleven years old. In the era when kids were smoking a little marijuana, she enrolled me in Synanon, a drug treatment program.

Her legacy was a lifetime of quasi-anorexia and a good Catholic loathing of our bodies. We were raised knowing that our worth depended on external features, what we looked like and what we accomplished. What happened on the inside? Irrelevant.

While everything I've done in my life since then has been in an effort to reconfigure this mindset, my mother's required practice of determined denial would serve me quite effectively on Day 3 of the Woodvale Challenge, and on Day 42, and every minute and hour and day in between.

FAMILIES ARE...INTERESTING

I married Alan at the age of twenty-four. None of the other graduate students were married. In retrospect, I was pretty naïve. His ex-wife and ex-girlfriend had warned me that he was "too nice to live with." But what was wrong with that? After a string of not-so-great boyfriends, I could live with a nice guy.

But Alan seemed depressed, and his elementary school aged son, too. Unconsciously, I felt they both needed saving. As a psychologist now, I understand my motivations: I couldn't save my mother or the unity of my first family, but by golly, I could love these two enough to make them all better. Alan and I lived together in my rented house. We got custody of Kurt because of familial problems, and so our family began even before we were married. Then we had a couple more wonderful children.

Alan and I divorced when my stepson was seventeen and the other two were eleven and thirteen. Joint custody of my children was devastating. I had never been significantly away from the younger two. My heart.

But we made it work. Despite the divorce, those kids and I spent a lot of quality time together. My rule for myself has always been that "If you are scared of something, you have to do it once. And then you have to do it again to prove that the first time was not a fluke of bravery." I seem to have passed this on to my children. They were my adventure buddies.

With my mantra as our guide, we did plenty of things that scared us—usually twice. Cliff diving, whitewater rafting, kayaking and canoeing, rock and mountain climbing. You name the adventure, we wanted to give it a try. We had a Hobie and I had bought the kids small sailboats, so we spent weekends and summers sailing. Each kid also had a horse to ride and care for. They were always involved in one activity or another along with at least one sport.

My daughter and I became close right from the start. As much as she was (and still is) clear and verbal about my failings as a parent (I think her list was originally called "The Five Betrayals," but I am sure it has grown since), it was all in good love. She was a lonely child, but a viciously determined and successful athlete and student, an athletic nerd. Our conventional middle school broke her heart, so she took off to an alternate high school where she was allowed to expand herself by taking college courses at Colorado University, where she studied Japanese and, at sixteen, went abroad to Japan. To this day, she is beautiful and accomplished and very sports oriented. She was my co-adventurer.

Although I encouraged her not to, my daughter matriculated at my prestigious alma mater, not as a legacy student but by her own merits. She became a crew star and worked her way nearly to the Olympic team, sacrificing much of her life for this endeavor until the Masters Nationals. She won, but snapped several ribs and tore cartilage. That injury destroyed her rowing career. Devastated by her loss, she turned herself into a rowing coach, a triathlete, a marathon runner, and a long -distance biker.

She and her partner (now wife) worked crazily. Her wife became a middle school teacher of science. My daughter inserted herself into Harvard as a lab manager and earned her doctorate in neurosciences there. She is now, apart from her athletic pursuits, a neuroscience and psychology professor, and they have two wonderful children.

And yes, for me, there was a new husband. I had known Mike in court where he presided as a judge and I testified (with my heart beating fast) as an expert witness. During his career, Mike had been an excellent public defender, then the head District Court judge in Boulder, Colorado. He later returned as a private defense attorney, then an international attorney. It was wonderful, finally, to spend time with someone who really seemed emotionally involved with me. It was kind of love/ passion at first sight. We were all really happy together.

ROWING? IN BOULDER?

All that family life did get in the way of my rowing career. I had rowed at Wellesley College, but there were quite a few years between that and getting into it again, which happened in a most unlikely place.

Boulder, Colorado, is exquisite, with its clear winter skies and sharply defined Rockies always in view, but it is difficult to be a waterbaby in the mountains. There just wasn't a lot of water available to please the eye and soothe the soul. We compensated by sailing our Hobie and sunfishes on the reservoir, whitewater rafting, and diving on vacation.

That all changed on a lovely spring day in 2000. There it was: two paragraphs in the *Boulder Daily Camera*, a call to all interested in rowing. I could not believe my eyes. My heart pounded. I guess I hadn't realized how much I missed being on the water until the possibility of it floated back into my life.

That weekend, I joined the mostly ex-East Coast crowd in a borrowed classroom at the Boulder Reservoir. The air buzzed with expectation. Since no one really knew anyone else, we were all mostly silent. Many in attendance were muscular and graceful, typical rower physiques.

Then Bob and Cymber Quinn strode out to the podium, and Bob stepped forward. "Greetings all, um, we're new here. We're just in from California, and we can't seem to find the boathouse." (loud laughter.)

He and his wife, Cymber, were proposing to form a rowing club at the reservoir for CU Athletics, with a private club for members. "We can build racks for oars and shells, organize teams and practices, set up some races. Anyone who wants to join pays a membership fee. Write your name here if you are interested."

Several of us squeaked with pleasure. I signed up.
Two weeks later, we met up in a slightly moldy and very chilly classroom, introduced ourselves, and talked about our rowing experiences. Most of us had rowed in college and/or boarding or private school (not uncommon in rowing worlds). The Quinns were willing to purchase two used eights, a four, and a double, and we would pay them back as a club through our membership fees. Rowers could also purchase their own boats and rent rack space. (Which I did. Immediately.) I guess it was my enthusiasm that landed me on the board of direc-tors..

With the Quinns as coaches, a group of us grew into Boulder Community Rowing. After gaining our certifications, we trained and coached novices. In no time I was engrossed in our rowing community. We all became friends and confidants and rowing partners.

I fell in love. As soon as the ice thawed in spring, nothing was more exquisite than shouldering the boat two by two ("All eight! Hands on!"), crunching across the rocks and sand, the ponderous weight of the shell digging indifferently into our calloused shoulders. The soft pine and humus breezes slid off the mountains to tease us, whispering "spring, spring, ssspp-rr-ing."

"Up and over head," the cox would call, then "into the water!" and we would swing the boat right side up and onto the lake. Oars, seat pads, sneakers in hand we would wade into the chilly mountain water, balance, step carefully onto the seat and slide down to seated position.

Finally: "Ready all? Row!" Just about every morning before the start of the workday, there we'd be, watching the sun rise across the plains and reflect on the mountains a warm, generous glow.

Boulder Community Rowing grew and evolved over the

years. We developed a racing team and a community rowing club. We traveled to different regattas, anywhere from San Diego to Northern California to the Masters National in Canada. We also were lucky enough to compete in a slew of regattas in the northeast, including the lofty Head of the Charles in Cambridge, Massachusetts. Before too long, we expanded our fleet. Many of us had our own shells, singles, pairs, even quads and fours. As with most rowing clubs, the members were warm, smart, determined, competitive and kind.

WHY PEOPLE DO WHAT THEY DO

In 2007, after a lot of encouragement and with some trepidation, my husband, Mike, left for the restoration of post-conflict Rule of Law in Liberia. I was very proud of the work he was doing as he trained judges, prosecutors and defense attorneys how to establish law in this civil war-ravaged country. But it was rough for me, due in part to poor communications from a nation at war, a circumstance which thrust us essentially into a non-relationship. What was supposed to be six months turned into three years with occasional visits. A gloom settled over me in our relationship.

Being immersed in a midlife crisis is depressingly trite.

By the time 2011 rolled around, I was fifty-eight and winter was coming. I stayed very busy, as usual, working as a clinical psychologist, renting out our seven-acre mountain property in Lyons, Colorado, and restoring a multi-family Victorian house in town. I moved into the second story apartment there and settled my office on the first floor.

Still, things were not working out well. One day, when I was supposed to be preparing for a client, our four golden retrievers and two cats sat staring at me as I stared out at the tree limbs beyond my window.

"Hey guys," I ruminated to the furry family, "what am I

going to do?"

No answer, only an ear prick of acknowledgement. What good were these guys, anyway?

Life did not feel smooth. Over the course of a year and a half, I broke first my arm and then my wrist, blowing any chance to row with my competitive team. They, in turn, were forced to move on without me. I felt weak and vulnerable and lost. I missed having family around.

But I worked. I loved my job. At that point my work as a Doctor of Psychology was multifold. I had a contract with Social Services to evaluate abused children and abusive/neglectful parents. It was endlessly fascinating, a window into the world of criminality and despair and damage and hurt. As I began to understand how these myriad experiences—many of them traumatic—all worked together, I started a Mother and Babies group to ensure maternal/infant bonding. But I also conducted a group for sex offenders. Primarily, though, I was a forensic psychologist either working in mitigation for death penalty cases or serious crimes, or evaluating victims regarding the impact of those crimes. I performed forensic psychological evaluations on people enduring domestic violence, on child abuse victims, and on abusers. I conducted and analyzed criminal and death row evaluations, spoke publicly about such topics as domestic violence, the impact of rape, and adolescent murderers. I ran workshops, working mostly with perpetrators and victims, and I felt honored to be a therapist to those in need.

Because I had been one of the first psychologists in the domestic violence movement, I had the opportunity early on to be the program director at a shelter for battered women. Doing so gave me the experience and insight I needed to train law enforcement, the public, and others on the crisis that is domestic violence.

What breathed life into me was the discovery of why people do what they do. Probing human nature was exciting and interesting, especially when my practice turned into predominantly forensic work, where psychology intersects with the law.

My life of adventure, however, became less satisfying. Forced by injuries to cox and not row, I was envious, angry, and hurt. I missed rowing in a visceral way. I tried bike riding, CrossFit (even becoming an instructor), and mini triathlons to distract me. My YMCA workout buddies and I did Super Saturdays packed with working out and long bike rides.

Mike was gone and the kids were all grown up. As my home emptied and I was left with a little too much time to think, those lifelong doubts about myself – Was I a good person? Attractive enough? Loved by my spouse? A good enough mother? – were like rats nibbling on my soul. Was I just another imposter? I needed something more.

THE SEED

I first heard about trans-ocean rowing from this guy, Dan. He'd come to the club at the end of the season, which was unconventional timing. And he was, in my eyes, a little weird. I remember when he showed up.

October 2010, the usual big sky crisp fall sunrise at the Boulder Community Rowing oar house, golden aspens shivering in the chill. The water was flat and smooth in the autumn splendor. We'd been alone on the water, as most boats were stored away for the season. Each of us exhaled little plumes of cloud as we climbed out of the eight and made ready to lift it out of the water.

"Hey, you guys," said Lauren, good friend and rowing coach, clicking off her phone.

"Any of you have any time? This guy wants to learn to row, and he can come down now."

One rower had to go to work. Seven rowers and a cox were

left waiting for Dan. We were all puzzled. Learn to row in October? So near the wintery end of the rowing season?

Tall, lanky, and more than a little awkward in his presentation, Dan finally arrived and lolled onto the dock, oar askew in his hand.

"Hey, Dan," we chorused. "Welcome."

Dan mumbled something. I don't know what exactly we were expecting, but not that.

"Ok folks," said Lauren, turning to Dan. "Let's get in the boat. Don't step on the floorboards, you can stick your foot right through a rowing shell."

We lowered ourselves in the boat first so we could hold it stable against the dock as Dan, all elbows and knees, stiffly stepped onto the seat and lowered himself down, then strapped his feet in the foot stretchers. Then plugged himself into his iPod.

Didn't take long to figure out what rowing was like with Dan. The guy kept his own rhythm to his own music. Our smooth collaborative ballet was marred by our butts to the kidneys and other offenses contrary to the harmony of rowing.

"Dan, Dan," coached patient Lauren, "you gotta try to stay in sync with the other rowers. Watch the stroke seat's shoulder and put your oar in exactly when she does."

In these sliding-seat rowing shells, the rowers face backwards toward the stern and pull the oars through the water. Seats are numbered One to Eight, with Seat One in the bow and Seat Eight, the stroke seat, in the stern facing the cox. Everyone keeps time with the stroke. That's key. The stroke is responsible for setting the pace and rhythm. The beauty of rowing happens when the other rowers follow in perfect synchronicity with Seat Eight. Rule #1 of rowing: you have to row in sync, and to do that, you follow the stroke.

Lauren's coaching fell on deaf ears. Dan rowed to his own drummer. Finally, it was over.

We were rowing in a sixty-foot 200-pound carbon fiber Schoenbrod 8+ shell – nothing too fancy, but we were proud to be able to row in it. Getting the boat out of the water was just the opposite of putting it in: you flip it up onto your shoulders and carry it, pair by pair, up the hill to the boathouse. That day, I was paired with Dan, who groused. The boat was heavy, he had stuff to do. You know.

I had to ask. "So hey, Dan, why are you learning to row now, with rowing season over for the year?"

Dan grunted under the weight of the boat and the hill climb. "I'm rowing the Atlantic in January for the Woodvale Challenge. They told me I should probably learn to row first."

"The Woodvale Challenge? What is that?"

There it was: the beginning of an adventure years in the unconscious making.

2

The Adventure Begins

THE WOODVALE ATLANTIC CHALLENGE

Dan's dream of racing across the Atlantic had piqued my curiosity in a big way. Of course, the Woodvale Challenge, as it turned out, was not for sissies.

Women before me had overcome societal obstacles, defied expectations, challenged the status quo, and embraced a spirit of curiosity and discovery. In 1901, Annie Edson Taylor, an American school teacher, on her sixty-third birthday became the first person to survive a trip over Niagara Falls in a barrel. Sylvia Earle, born in 1935, became a world renown expert on marine biology and the first woman to lead the National Oceanic and Atmospheric Administration (NOAA), and holds the record for the deepest walk on the sea floor. In 1963, in the Vostok 6, Valentina Tereshkova was the first woman to fly into space. While I cannot compare myself to any of them, the list of women heroes is long yet relatively unknown.

That night, after that strange man had planted an interesting idea in my hungry heart, I did some research. Wikipedia describes ocean rowing as "the sport of rowing across oceans." Go figure. It is considered to be "an extreme psychological and physical challenge." To qualify as an ocean row, the rows must be "unassisted," meaning any assistance at all disqualifies the row. (In fact, in an emergency, assistance would be twenty-four to forty-eight hours away.) As of 2024, fewer people had rowed an ocean than had climbed Mount Everest or free-dived the deep and deadly tunnel in southeast Sinai known as "the Arch."

How could I resist? I called Woodvale for more information.

Kate, the then-manager, was completely encouraging.

"I like your style!" she chirped in clipped British. "Would you be interested in rowing a single across the Atlantic? You could break a record!"

Grinning out at the brittle pre-winter morning in Colorado, I laughed. "Not on your life. Me? Alone? Never." (Okay, maybe not *never*.) "But please do send more information? I might be interested in the race. I mean, on a racing *team*."

Then I sat back and examined my motives.

• Always up for a challenge. Sure, this may be the biggest one I ever tackled (other than childbirth), but why not? People do it all the time. Sort of.

• The kids were well launched and doing fine. They didn't need me.

• Mike. Well, Mike.

• I could prove my mettle to myself.

• What else was there to do?

That settled it. Yes, I know, it helped to have Midge hissing in my ear, *I didn't raise you to be a sissy…You'll finally be skinny… Of course you're going to do this…You have to.*

Thing is, it is with great wistfulness that I admit I never have been, am not now, and never will be a real athlete. I know it sounds completely badass, this fifty-eight-year-old woman jumping into a boat with thirteen hardbodied super-jocks (they weren't, but a girl can dream), but I'm really just kind of wiry and intellectual. I do participate in all kinds of athletic endeavors – CrossFit, triathlons – but generally with only dogged and tenacious mediocrity.

I also break things. Bones mostly. I have been casted and stitched up more than most. When I was eight, I stumbled carrying a plastic Breyer horse and came home with one of its hooves stuck in my eyebrow, necessitating removal and repair of the horse dangling from my forehead. The next year, I fell playing kickball, and three stones embedded themselves in my knee, requiring medical excision. When I watched the procedure with great interest and no whimpering, the surgeon determined that I appeared "cognitively slow." My senior year of high school was spent in a leg cast from sticking a bare foot through the spokes of my speeding bicycle.

I hesitate to say I am clumsy, but I would venture a guess that I am not always great at paying attention, especially when I'm trying to make my non-athletic self do more than it was designed to do. But it's not entirely my own fault. Genetics also plays a defining role in my lack of athleticism. My people are better suited for picking potatoes or mashing grapes. And drinking. Strong Irish/Italian loading on the wine factor.

Later that evening, a call came. It was Kate, a little

breathless with excitement.

"Suzanne!! So glad I caught you! Woodvale is organizing a women's crew to become the first women's six to row the Atlantic. You could even make a time record!"

"Me?" I stuttered.

"Yes, YOU. I loved chatting with you the other night! I like your competitive spirit and I think you would be so right for the position." She paused at the other end of the line, like maybe she was rallying for the win. "Are you interested in being interviewed for a seat in the boat?"

Was this really happening? I was stunned by the gathering momentum of this trip. Yes, it was intriguing, and I was never opposed to tackling the big challenges. And I could use the distraction, something new to focus on. Suddenly, the Woodvale Challenge became something I could do for me to be me.

"I guess so. Okay."

The next day, I received an email from Kate.

Suzanne,

In a polite way...I have worked out that you will be the oldest female ever to row across the Atlantic (current record holder was 55) so potentially three records in the bag for you!

Kind regards

Kate Battes

Events Director

www.woodvale-challenge.com

A little history: In the first Atlantic Rowing Race, in 1997, thirty teams of courageous individuals set out into the unknown to row across the Mid-Atlantic route, from Tenerife, Spain, to Barbados. In 2005, Ben Fogle and James Cracknell famously competed in the race, bringing the world of ocean rowing into the spotlight. Since then, there had been (as of 2011) a further five races across this same route, with more than 240 individuals taking on the challenge, successfully joining the elite few known as Ocean Rowers.

Ocean Rowing: The concept of ocean rowing was born whenChay Blyth and John Ridgway crosed the Atlantic in 1966. The first Atlantic Rowing Race was organized in 1997. Now, decades later, over one thousand determined people have achieved the ultimate in human endeavors.

Trans-Atlantic rowing races, usually from the Canary Islands to the Caribbean, take several weeks and can be grueling. Crews often row in shifts, burning 5,000–8,000 calories per day. The mental strain is as tough as the physical, and the risks are many and varied. Storms can wreak havoc, flooding or even capsizing a boat. Rowers are subject to sores of all kinds, dehydration, sunburn, sleep deprivation. There are always encounters with large ships, marine wildlife, and rogue waves, and rescues not only disqualify the boat, but can be extremely difficult.

Under the guidance of Simon Chalk (who himself held nine Guinness records including "First ever person to row solo across the Indian Ocean"), Woodvale was the foremost builder of ocean rowing boats and the sponsor of the Woodvale Atlantic Challenge. The 2011 race was to start in the Spanish port of San Sebastian de la Gomera in the Canary Islands and follow what's known as the Columbus route, westbound across the mid-Atlantic to Port St. Charles in Barbados.

Ridiculous! How in the world could this fifty-eight-year-old woman possibly survive this ridiculous escapade, labeled by many as The World's Toughest Rowing Race?

Worried about leaving my work and my home for essentially two months, I called Mike in Africa, and explained the whole story.

"Wow, that sounds incredible, of course we can subsidize it. If that is really what you want to do, then I say you should do it."

Relieved but still uncertain, I dialed my daughter. She screamed with excitement. "Ma! You gotta do it! I'd go with you but I can't but you have to do it."

After I hung up the phone, my head filled with doubts and anxiety. Wasn't this risky? What is wrong with these people? Doesn't any of them have an iota of sense? Not one person in my family voiced concern or tried to dissuade me. Where was the "Oh Mommy, please don't go, we need you. It's too dangerous" that I had half-expected? I guess all that adventure parenting had sunk in pretty deep. Well, this was my chance to really and truly walk the talk, more vigorously than I'd ever imagined.

Finally, I called Kate and broke the news. "I'm in."

Kate's voice burbled with excitement. "That's the spirit, Suzanne. It's going to be an incredible adventure."

She had no idea. Neither did I.

The next day I called my sister Debbie. Finally, the voice of reason: she burst into tears.

"If you die I'm going to kill you," she sobbed.

"Debbie, where were you when I needed you to talk me out of it?"

She was too busy crying to answer. I guess that was why I didn't call her first.

CROCS AND COCONUT OIL

Since the 1970s and the era of the Women's Movement, a diverse set of female endurance athletes have been spawned. While I'll have more to report below, by 2021, fewer than two hundred women had successfully rowed an ocean. Among recent notables is Jasmine Harris who, in 2021, won the distinction of being the youngest female to row solo across the ocean, in 70 days, 3 hours and 48 minutes. In 2024, Lauren Champion and Li Roland set a new world record as the fastest women's pair, accomplishing the feat in 45 days, 1 hour and 27 minutes. These unstoppable women show us what is possible if we work together and believe in ourselves.

Woodvale made its announcement:

- Lia Ditton (30), a professional sailor from Portsmouth, England – this would be her second ocean row

- Anna Lewis (26), a graduate student at Oxford

- Anne Marie Chouinard (32), a consultant from Massachusetts, USA

- Jennifer Weterings (41), a Health Services Manager from Vancouver, Canada

- Suzanne Pinto (57), a psychologist from Boulder, USA, and the oldest woman ever to row an ocean

- Julia Immonen (31), a Sky Sports News production assistant from London and the first Finnish person ever to row an ocean.

The November sun set early over the Rocky Mountains. I was trying to work on a report in my comfy if slightly musty therapist office, dogs at my feet, cat on my lap. I'd always been pretty good at compartmentalizing, but this Woodvale craziness was becoming so distracting that when I could manage to focus on work, I took full advantage of the brain space. My clients needed me.

The moment of peace and productivity was fleeting.

Into my inbox popped a message from Lia Dutton.

"Cheers, crew! I am your captain on our six-woman crossing. Having rowed the Atlantic prior I know what to expect."

Excellent. We would have an experienced captain and cox. The relief that washed over me made me realize how anxious I had been in the face of the unknown.

"I have written up a list of preparatory items. Here are all the things you must eat to get your body ready." She called it the "Build-Up Diet":

• Coconut oil, non-hydrogenated. Spread thickly on rye bread, use in stir-fries. Aim to have at least one tablespoon a day.

• Tahini. Use as a dip, sandwich filler or as a filling for baked potatoes.

• Hummus. Use as a dip, sandwich filler, on top of rice cakes topped with plenty of sprouts (sprouted alfalfa, lentils, sunflower seeds, mung and chickpeas).

• Guacamole. Use as a dip, lavish on top of salad.

• At least one avocado a day. This is good build up food at 400 calories a time.

• Pumpkin seed butter. Use liberally.

• Plenty of oily fish, sweet potato mash, squash and pumpkin.

She told us to start each day with porridge made with soy or oat milk and sprinkled with plenty of raw nuts and seeds for added protein. She encouraged flaxseed oil, all kinds of nuts and grains (quinoa, millet, and buckwheat), and a selection of fermented foods (tempeh, natto and miso). We were to avoid too much salt. Also:

• Eat generous amounts of the green food powder, wheatgrass, green barley, blue green algae, spirulina.

- Eat a handful of goji berries.

- Eat lots of fresh vegetable soups with plenty of beans and pulses. Soup is already partially broken down so it should be easy to digest.

- Eat organic free-range eggs. Have them boiled or poached. This is a form of easily digested protein and a good source of lecithin.

Ugh – a very Boulder diet. Was she working for Whole Foods? I had never even tasted a lot of this stuff. Goji Berries? Green Food powder? I decided to stick to my paleo diet of vegetables, fruit, meat and fish...and coffee and wine of course.

She ended her initial instructions with another list. "Crew, these are essentials that you must bring on the trip. Keep in mind though, we cannot bring too much." We would be allowed only ten pounds of gear, including:

- iPod ($249 x 5?)

- iPod speakers - got 'em!

- iPod armbands ($14.95 x 6)

- Chargers (iPod, laptop, cameras—everything)

- Waterproof headphones ($33 x 6)

- Video camera

- Water leash ($12)

- Memory cards ($50 x 4)

- GoPro Fisheye cameras (Can I get these for free? Working on it.)

- Tripods and brackets ($20 x 2)

- X-Gate software (Sponsored? Working on it.)

- Batteries

- Inverter ($20)

- Walkie-talkies ($40 x 2)

I expected the email thread to blow up with panicked questions, but my inbox stayed almost eerily quiet. There were a few questions and "get-to-know-you" queries, but they went unanswered. Lia, we were discovering, barely had time for us. Still, we were all a little in awe of a prior Atlantic rower.

I did react a little to this tidbit:

"A women's boat requires a great deal of emotional processing and hand-holding..."

What? I muttered at the computer with a glare. Stereotype much? That's when it first occurred to me that the social aspect of this stuff might be more challenging than any of the physical hardships we were about to endure. Well, it's whatever, I told myself. You wanted a challenge, you're getting one.

We would also need two t-shirts, two pairs of running shorts, and two pairs of wool socks. Pretty efficient, right? We'd share everything else, like dry shampoo and toothpaste. This made me laugh. I don't even like camping because I hate going without a shower. And I cannot even imagine an hour, let alone a day, without reading a book. An actual book, like with pages to turn. This project was certainly stretching my norms. That said, I was psyched. I put everything I could find on my credit card and had it shipped to me in Boulder.

A serious topic of online conversation ensued involving footgear for the crossing. Anyone who has used a rowing machine at a gym is aware that the feet are held onto the foot stretchers by a single strap across the top of the foot. But, as Lia noted, "the chafing of that strap during endless hours of rowing can cause serious wounds to the feet. What are our alternatives?"

Suzanne: "What about sneakers? Would they be protective?"

Jennifer: "Water shoes, definitely."

Julia: "I'd vote for Birkenstocks. They've never failed me yet."

We debated.

"Absolutely no sneakers," Lia wrote. "I refuse to have seven pairs of wet, stinking, moldering sneakers on deck."

A collective sigh.

"What about Crocs?" I ventured. "It's a rubber shoe with a hard top and holes to allow your feet to breathe. I saw online that they now make a furry insert, sort of like bedroom slippers."

A collective hesitation. Then Lia settled it.

"Sounds great! Can we do that? Suzanne, isn't Crocs based in Boulder? See if you can get us a sponsorship."

"Yeah, and maybe shoes for the guys as well..."

Things were starting to feel pretty good. I was excited, and I already felt a part of this endeavor having a job that allowed me to contribute to this trip of ours. I felt like I had a goal and a purpose.

Of course, then there was a flurry of emails to get everyone's sizes, then discussions with the Crocs company. The wonderful people there ended up sending us fourteen pairs of Crocs for our journey, black hard-shelled exteriors with lush bedroom slipper inserts. In exchange, they requested only updates and information. So many good folks in the world.

3

Sharks Don't Bite Through Boats

A month later, I felt half imposter and half adventurer taking myself to Portsmouth, England, to become an ocean rower. According to Kate, "In order to be allowed to depart from the Canary Islands we are required to pass all of these courses and show certifications. This is a portion of the coursework for a Sea Captain certification." We were there for training.

Now, I'm a good student, always have been, so coursework was never scary. But I couldn't ignore the reality that this was just prep for something a lot bigger. I'll admit to some trepidation. Who was I to think I could handle any of this, much less win a giant race and break all kinds of records? To be honest, I didn't doubt my strength and fitness. I could kick this race's ass...right? What I may have lacked in muscle, I knew I more than made up for in spirit and stamina, my trademark take-no-prisoner's tenacity, maybe just an outright unwillingness to fail.

But that was outward-facing Pinto. In the dark hours, the inner playground bully whispered nasty nothings in my ear. *You really think you can keep up with these women? I guarantee not one of them ever had a plastic horse embedded in her forehead. There aren't enough pushups in the world that could bring you to their level. They're going to curse you for slowing them down...You're going to lose this race for them...*

Two more obstacles:

• I am really shy. I can play the extrovert, but it's all an act and completely exhausting.

• What the heck is with these Brits? I can hardly understand a word they're saying.

Heathrow was a wild buzz of languages, sweat, food and hurry. Where was I supposed to go? How was I supposed to find anything? I spun in my spot. Eventually, I was rescued by two smiling women, Anne Marie and Jen, striding up the corridor, waving. With great confidence they wove their way through the fluorescent jungle. Anna would be waiting outside to take us all to a rower's house in Portsmouth.

After seven years of graduate school in psychology and decades of practice, I knew the interpersonal stuff would have a real impact on the trip. I recognized the importance of first impressions and starting off on the right foot. I was also just really curious. And nervous.

It soon became clear that Anna, Oxford scholar and former rower, knew just about everything. Her plump body bedecked in skirts and scarves, she was peaches and cream personified. She was a Dresden doll of an Englishwoman with dark curly hair spilling out from under whatever brimmed hat she wore to protect her unmarred skin. Her layers and leggings worked perfectly for her.

Anna: Underlying all that sweet femininity, Anna turned out to be astonishingly capable and competent. At that point, in addition to training for a trans-Atlantic rowing adventure, she was working on a PhD (after two Masters, one in physics) at Oxford. Quiet but very sure of herself, deeply kind, and supremely logical, Anna took charge of mentoring us through all the courses, and we came to rely on her. Dependable Anna. Anna the Girl Scout. I suspected she scared young men a bit, with her precision and sharp intelligence.

As we squeezed into the tiny coupe, sharing space with a whole lot of luggage, I couldn't help but continue a little analysis of my teammates. Anne Marie, a fellow American, appeared to be more hesitant, plain in demeanor and speech. Tall and brown-haired, she struck me as fit, but not superhuman. I felt we both were on the normal side of the fitness spectrum. She was bright in an intellectual way. We spoke of Boston and people we know in common in the rowing world, and those connections brought us together. I liked Anne Marie, although her anxiety peeked through early on.

Jen: reserved, content to listen, chiming in only occasionally about her Vancouver Island solo rows. Jen looked fit, especially if one observed her bikini body. She came across as strong and competent, self-assured, an athlete.

We were to be trained in South Hampton by KTY Yachts, specialists in Marine training and offshore survival courses. Every day, we'd pile into the car to drive an hour for a day-long grind in order to eventually graduate and reassure the Spanish government that we were safe to embark. The venue was a typical boatyard, congested with nautical piles and boats awkwardly on stands. November gloom–which, in England, can get mighty gloomy–made the surroundings chilly and morose. Boat workers hammered and drilled.

- Thursday, 9 December - Sea Survival

- Friday, 10 December - First Aid at Sea

- Saturday-Wednesday, 11-15 December - Ocean Yacht-master

- Thursday, 16 December - VHF Radio

- Friday-Saturday, 17-18 December - Practice Row from Southampton to Weymouth

The training was, to be honest, overwhelming. It was also fascinating celestial navigation, VHF radio, parachute anchors, and first aid. We practiced jumping from a high board with a life jacket and flipping over and climbing in and out of lifeboats...in a pool. But survival out there, in the open ocean? Movies about ocean-goers lost at sea and sea rescues by helicopter were just a little too close for comfort.

"What about sharks?" Anne Marie quavered. "I am so afraid of sharks."

"Sharks don't bite through boats," I lied.

Jen also turned out to harbor an insecurity or two. When we walked at lunch, she shared her angst about unrequited love. We shared puffs on secret cigarettes and sips of wine. I thought we were becoming friends. But then she started to make more strategic alliances, particularly with the male crew members. By mid-week, the whole scene started to feel like a season of *Survivor.* The training had become an ordeal.

Throughout the course, Anna was our genius, tutoring us far into the night on how to graph our routes should the automatic pilot fail. There, in the dingy, threadbare living room of our rental, we'd hunch over the maps, graph paper and compass in hand. Dim memories of high school geometry and algebra haunted the periphery of my dull brain.

"Suzanne? Do you want me to help you?"

"Oh, Anna," I sighed. "Good luck with that. The tide will push us to Barbados before I could plot a true course. Math is my rubicon."

"Not to worry." She was so good. "You can do this."

"I don't know, Anna. What if I can't?" What was so weird is that I'm not a can't person. Was there something else going on? "This stuff is so difficult for me. I wonder if they will just send me home."

Anna laughed. "Nope. No way. That's not how it works." Her certainty helped a lot. And this one thing became clearer every day: questioning ourselves was a big fat waste of time. I am afraid to admit that organizer Lia Dutton had been right about emotional processing and hand-holding. I don't know, maybe the same shit goes on with men—yeah, yeah, the binary is just a social construct—but damn. I guess strength doesn't mean confidence, and confidence is relative.

Even in a boat full of women about to row the Atlantic, insecurities arise.

Anne Marie got the ball rolling. One night, as we wandered around a suburban neighborhood, the air cool and fresh, houses tidy and asleep, she commenced the agonizing.

"Nobody really takes me seriously," she moaned. "I'm really scared of sharks and rogue waves. They are real!" She stopped and turned to me, her whole body tensed and explosive.

"We all watched the Rescue at Sea films - that made me very anxious. I just don't think you guys understand how frightening and realistic it all is."

It wasn't just about the sharks. A week in, and tensions among the crew were becoming palpable as we tried to figure ourselves out. But she wanted to talk about her feelings.

I listened. "Oh, Anne Marie, of course we understand...
this is quite an undertaking. Of course the movies were scary,
but also in some ways exhilarating, right? Besides, you can't get
all besotted with negative 'what ifs?....'" By the time we headed
for bed, I think she was feeling better.

THE FIRST TO GO

We graduated! We were ready to do this thing. Simon tucked
our certificates away.

Simon Chalk was captaining an all-men crew, and we had
fun with them as well. We invited a couple of them over to
dinner and went out a couple of times with the entire group. I
was surprised at how hard it was to break through the surface
with them. They were all perfectly decent men, but I believe
their own anxieties isolated them. They laughed about the rumors from the women's quarters about our emotional processing, but my guess is that they were going through a lot of the
same stuff and envied our ability to do so openly. Truth be
known, we were a team so we had to check in with each other,
but we definitely didn't get to really know each other. Yet.

On our last day in South Hampton, Kate, all energy and
bustle, charged into the room.

"Lia is pulling out of the race. Her sponsor didn't come
through." She scanned our shocked faces.

"What do you guys want to do, scratch the race? Fun while
it lasted?"

"Scratch it? You are totally kidding!" We were horrified.

"So what, then?" In Jen's stance, a challenge. "Are we going to give it all up? Or are we

game to go, just us?" Anne-Marie's eyes were saucers. "Do
you think we really could do it?" She shook her head, probably
involuntarily.

Oh no you don't. "Look, guys," I was in full-on coach mode, "we have spent a lot of money and time to get this far, and it would be a disaster to just let it go. All we need is a new captain. I say we go."

Jen agreed. "I say we go."

Three of us nominated Anne Marie, the most practical of the group, to be our captain.

Jen was miffed. "I'm the only one of us with coastal rowing experience. I did a solo journey through the Vancouver Islands. I think I should be captain."

How to put it gently? I knew honesty was key here, but this stuff was tricky. How to explain that the fact that Jen was annoyed here was a good example of why we wanted to go with even-tempered Anne-Marie instead? Maybe we could skip the explanation part, just this once.

It was decided, then.

"We got this," we exalted. "First five-woman crew."

Anne Marie added, "And another new world record."

Then Julia dropped out. We were down to four.

MEN!

Our last day in England was fraught with worry and distress. The race was paid for, we'd earned our certificates—there really was no going back. But then...

Some more rowers had dropped out of the men's boat. Simon was wavering.

We were all angry, indignant, and scared. Here we were, forced to make a decision while still in the boatyards of the training facility. Simon's goal was for us to break the world record and cross the ocean in 42 days. Everything was upended. Simon's only options would be to combine the men's boat and the women's boat—fourteen in all—or don't go at all.

The (First) Crew

- Captain Simon Chalk
- First mate Roger
- Colin
- Mike
- Nabs
- Dan
- Shaun
- Ben
- Guy
- Jamie (replaced by Jonathan)
- Anne Marie (replaced by Beth)
- Jen
- Anna
- Suzanne

I imagined our boat, built for ten-twelve rowers at most. Where would the extra people sleep? What would happen in the off-hours? How would the extra weight slow us down? Wave after wave of doubt washed over me. Was I really willing to spend thirty-three days (our revised goal given the extra manpower) in a tiny boat with thirteen other sweaty smelly cranky humans? Including men?

What about the unpleasant reality that most male ocean rowers, to minimize chafing, row naked?

What about the utter lack of privacy of relieving oneself in a bucket in full view of both men and women?

The whole experience had changed. I fretted. Captain Simon gave us till departure to decide. The pressure was on.

I complained via email to a good friend and rowing buddy in Colorado, Jennifer, who encouraged me. "You are where you are meant to be."

Shit. Why was I meant to be in a boat at sea, pooping in front of the entire co-ed crew?

We received our Certificates of Achievement and prepared to head out, to pass the time before the race back in the familiar comfort of our own homes. We were all too torn apart to warmly hug our goodbyes. Glumly mulling over the decision, we gathered in the shabby living room of our week-long home, deflated. At last, Jen sighed and called for a vote.

"Yay or nay?" she said. "Go with the guys or go home?"

Filled with doubt and reluctance, I quavered, "If we go home we will have wasted all of

our money and time, not to mention giving up the adventure. I say we go."

"Anyone can drop off and anyone can go," says Anna. "Looks like Pinto is in. Who else?"

Anne Marie appeared lost in thought, but then she murmured, "I think we should go."

The vote was unanimous. All four agreed–reluctantly–to go as a joint boat.

We heard later that in the next room, the men were having the same doubts.

"Simon!" Anne Marie called out, "We are going! Now what?"

✦

Two days later, back in my office in Boulder, yawning over my coffee and getting ready for work, I opened an email from Kate.

Dear *Brittania III* crew:

I hope you all are at home and doing well, preparing for the Challenge in every way you can. I regret to inform you that

due to a sudden back injury Anne Marie has opted out of the
Challenge. I understand that this may cause inconvenience
to the crew but her welfare is our greatest concern.

We are making every effort to find a qualified replacement
for Anne Marie. We will keep you apprised of any develop-
ments in that regard,...

Ah, the tornado of emails between the rest of us, wondering if Anne Marie's fears got the best of her.

"I will miss her," I said.

Jen was straightforward about it. "It is better she make the
choice now, when she can, rather than suffer her fears or an
injury."

Kate chimed in, "I am a little surprised they want to get
a replacement for Ann Marie rather than just go with three
women...maybe it is a financial decision."

No doubt. Or was someone superstitious? We went with
fourteen.

GOODBYES

At first, things felt like they were moving fast. We were to meet
in Tenerife, Canary Islands, on January 1, 2011, for a departure date two weeks later–give or take. Simon had figured in
two weeks of boat preparation in Tenerife, although the actual
departure date would depend on the weather.

Ocean rowing on the Atlantic is, by necessity, constrained
to the winter months, i.e. anything that isn't hurricane season.
This is approximately December through April. While we were
given instruction on how to avoid a hurricane (row hard the
other way), we were not eager to meet one in the middle of the
Atlantic.

My Colorado rower friends were supportive and loving.
Cinda and Jennifer gave me waterproof notebooks and pens.

Shawna lent me her travel pillow and her talisman that had accompanied all of her adventures. Julie designed a shirt that proclaimed "less than 45" (days).

I laughed. "I hope people don't think I'm talking about my age."

I was able to notify all of my clients and referral agencies that I would likely be gone for more than three months and was fortunate to find backups for some of the more fragile folks.

I started my journal, vowing to write daily.

As usual, my family headed south to our home in Mexico for Christmas. Wine time, out on the back balcony scanning the beach for my kids swimming in the Sea of Cortez. Our two-story Mediterranean-style home, red-tile-roofed and white-walled, was balconied and windowed all around so as never to lose sight of the cerulean sky and sapphire ocean, a scene punctured enthusiastically and all day long by hundreds of head-on divers, hungry brown pelicans.

Usually pretty well protected by a tumbled rock breakwater, our place provided a calm launch for kayaks or paddleboards. Honeymoon Island, a sandbar of saguaros and gulls, peregrine and pelican nests, was some distance away (though my daughter once swam it, with me behind in a kayak safety boat, gasping "cold, cold, cold" with every stroke in the winter sea). Our cove curved, so we could see all the way to the seaport to the east and to the iconic 1000-foot peaks of Tetakawi to the west.

Adopted desert plants flowered vivaciously in Talavera pots lining the courtyards and cobblestone streets of our small town, fireworks of reds, purples, magentas, and yellows.

Sonoran high desert tumbled to the sea filled with limbed sahuaros, palo verdes, and ocotillo.

It looked like Beirut, Mike said.

San Carlos was our home and our paradise, and that last

week there, with the family and the dogs and the sunshine, was perfection. I felt good and strong and happy, self-confident in a new way, as if I had a secret self that no one really needed to know about. I was working out hard, too, and all the men in the gym asked who was the crazy old lady who worked out so fervently. I had this big thing I was doing, but, for some reason, I felt no compulsion to talk a lot about it.

Christmas morning, we gathered around the fake tree tenderly decorated with ornaments chosen by my children every year since their birth. Yes, some were getting a little mangled, some slightly tattered. But truly, they all went perfectly with the moth-eaten artificial branches and needles. The kids were adults now, but there was still something special about hanging these treasures, each one infused with memories, reasons to laugh, or sometimes cry.

The ritual began with a free-for-all stocking-gift reveal. After that, each of us around the circle opened one present at a time, always allowing plenty of room for admiration and cheers. My Christmas gifts would sustain me on my journey. My daughter and her wife presented me with a waterproof book of photos of family, furry and otherwise. I cried, accepting and reveling in their love and pride. From my son, a St. Christopher's medal. I wept again. St. Christopher had historically been the saint of travelers until the Catholic church ousted him for not performing enough or any miracles.

Love and hugs and kisses all around. Almost everyone vowed to meet the boat in Barbados. Except for Mike. "Why would I do that?" he asked, but it wasn't a question. I was pretty confused by that, and a little forlorn. Yes, he had recently returned from Liberia, and yes, he was financially supportive and willing to take care of the dogs. But I wondered if three years apart had taken their toll.

In any case, I was ready to go.

PART TWO

Before

4

A Long Trip to the Starting Line

The trip to La Gomera was long long long. From San Carlos, my daughter, Regan, and her wife, Cindy, drove me north to Tucson. The border crossing was easy – twenty minutes – but it still took six hours to get to the airport hotel in town. We were all quiet, tired, and a little strained.

In Tucson, we did some last-minute shopping (how did I still need a water bottle?) then went to the movies (*The Black Swan* – not so great), then to dinner at California Pizza Kitchen (again, not so great). Perhaps we were just feeling a little overwhelmed.

At the mall, my daughter parked the car at what looked like six miles from the entrance to REI. Impatient, I whined, "Honey, would it be too hard to park a little closer?"

"How are you going to row across an ocean," she snapped back, "if you can't walk across a parking lot?"

Ouch. I wanted to joke that "I am conserving my strength," but no one seemed to be in the mood to laugh.

She dropped me at the Tucson Airport at 3:30 a.m. But just when I got into the line to check luggage, I heard "Ma, Ma!" There was my statuesque redhead sprinting the length of the airport, my left-behind coffee in hand.

"I love you, Babydoll." I hugged her tight, one last time.

"I love you, Ma. Be careful."

Thus began a marathon series of flights to Denver, Dulles, Madrid, and then several hours waiting for a plane to Tenerife South, in the Canary Islands. I tried to sleep, nearly impossible.

Finally, through the plane window, there she was. Parades of whitewashed and tan condos high up the mountain cascaded towards the beach, sort of California beach-town-ish, without much regard for the landscaping. Little restaurants, I would soon learn, lined the one main street. What it lacked in charm, Tenerife made up for in climate perfection–not too hot, and the sea was calm as a lake.

At the airport, I was lucky enough to meet up with Ben.

Ben: Very British and red-headed, Ben was as white as an egg and fearful of being bitten by the sun. An accountant by trade, he managed the finances for several families including the Legos. Although his accent was a bit hard to understand at first, he came across right away as quick, analytical and bright.

"Hullo!" he called out. "Suzanne, right? Are we to share a cabbie for the docks?" He seemed to have a lot of energy. "We have a bit of time before the ferry takes off. Care to take in a pub? Have a pint and a bit to eat, shouldn't we?"

"You read my mind!" We flagged a taxi.

At the ferry dock, we stowed our suitcases at the offices, changed into shorts, and walked across the long empty beach back to town. The ferry to our ultimate destination, La Gomera, would arrive in a couple of hours.

Ben found us a pub (finally, I was starving), and I guzzled a couple of glasses of wine which, in light of the lack of food, was probably not prudent. Ben was articulate and intelligent, lovely to talk with. We had fun getting to know each other better. Would everything be this easy?

Nope. After a leisurely stroll back to the ferry, I realized my camera was gone. Shoot, a rough start. Then, in mining my purse for any sign of it, I knocked my new sunglasses off the pier. Fortunately, there was a ledge below that caught them, but I felt very foolish and wondered if my stumbling was a result of drink or just utter exhaustion. I'd left Mexico thirty-one hours before.

I clambered down to the ledge to retrieve my shades. Now about that camera. In what would probably be a vain effort, we made a circuit back up the beach towards town. I was pessimistic. It wasn't on the beach, and I didn't want to go all the way back into town.

"Oh, Ben, I give up." I sighed. "What a bad start to this trip."

But Ben insisted. "C'mon, what do we have to lose?" I have to admit, I was starting to really admire this very kind, very energetic fellow. If every guy on the boat was this pleasant, we'd have a great time.

We began again, our eyes sweeping the sand. And then, remarkably–

"Ben! Look!!"

Lo and behold, there it was, propped atop a soda can by a good Samaritan, my brand-new Nikon. Unbelievable, and another warm and happy sign about the goodness of others.

The last leg of the journey, from Tenerife to La Gomera, was a forty-minute ride on an ornate and gleaming ferry. We both totally crashed in the semi-comfortable chairs.

"Yo! Hullo!" hollered Ben as we arrived at the final ferry terminal. "Anna and Kate!"

We'd be staying at various apartments around town, the women in a two-bedroom. I'd share a room with Anna, and Jen and whomever Kate had found as a replacement would share the other.

Kate was all business. "Let's hurry a bit, so we are not late for the reunion and our meeting at the Blue Marlin."

Ah yes, the Blue Marlin. Infamous rower bar. We really had arrived.

LA GOMERA

January 5

Wow, totally crashed and slept till 8:30.

I'm so happy to be getting back to journaling. I'm going to keep such a detailed record of this trip that I'll never forget a single moment of it. I can already feel how writing it down calms me. It always has.

La Gomera, like Tenerife and like St. Thomas in the U.S. Virgin Islands, is a mountain in the sea — all vertical, though unlike the Virgin Islands, this ambitious archipelago is more brown than green, dominated by Mount Teide, a dormant volcano and Spain's highest peak. The towns here are much smaller than in most of the Caribbean, but the chichi Spanish style has more of a big city vibe, rich and poor combined, *glittering tourist hotels next to bustling supermercados. The cobblestone streets are alive with the clacking of townspeople "doing the paseo," hugging and greeting friends and neighbors as they stroll around the Centro.*

Humans share the town square with clowders of semi-feral cats, fed and cared for by the townspeople. Their presence created a warm, comfortable snuggery at the town center.

Simon had managed to find a replacement for Anne Marie without too much trouble. Beth, from Cleveland, was attractive, early-forties-ish, perfectly pleasant. Also weirdly indolent, which was disconcerting. Jobless, divorced and looking, Beth marched to her own set of drums. She was not the only woman to do this kind of life-changing reinvention-y trip post-break-up. I'm sure it was something about wanting to find herself or perhaps some greater meaning.

Was I also looking for greater meaning? Oh come on, we all were.

Beth resisted our efforts to connect, but is that so surprising? Rowing really is, for many, an individual sport. So she passed up her chance to come out to breakfast with Anna and me, *bocadillos de jamon y queso y un café*. Maybe she knew what we hadn't figured out yet: this was going to be a long trip, plenty of together time.

> **Beth** hadn't spoken to her mother in forever, and her father scorned her going on this trip. She would have no one to meet her in Barbados, which would be sadder if she were a more sympathetic person and less of a caricature. On the other hand, she was definitely an "expert" on rowing. It amazed me that such a soft person could pull so hard on the oar. I wish now I had been able to know her better.

Starting right then. After breakfast, we all made our way down to the dock to meet the *Brittania III* and get to work sanding oars, taping oars, painting oars, measuring oars, putting collars on the oars. It was a good long enterprise of hard work.

The guys on our crew were lovely. If they weren't so dry, one might absolutely want to marry a Brit. They were all so helpful, so polite, naturally engaging and supportive. In fact, our team was starting to feel like a therapy group. It reminded me of this dive bar in Longmont named "Group Therapy."

Speaking of bars, the clear highlight of every day was hitting one and joining all of the secret smokers. We mostly hung out at the Blue Marlin, where rower paraphernalia bedecked the walls and the conversations always came back to everyone's favorite topic.

One afternoon a few days in, I was greeted by the delightful bald-headed bartender.

"Hey lady," he yelled out when I waltzed in, "you walked out without paying your bill last night…Whenever you can! I know you will be back!"

I wondered for a brief second whether I should cut back a little on the alcohol. Nah.

Our first big crew meeting happened at the place next door. It was exciting and scary to realize that, with Simon on board, expectations were high. We had moved from just trying to make it across the ocean to a world of sophisticated rowing technology and meticulously organized expectations. Now we were talking about the trim of the boat, weight of rowers, seating positions, rowing shifts, timing, and more. It was exciting and gratifying to be learning from the master of ocean rowing. I thought we'd been determined before, but this was a whole new world of purpose and resolve.

Simon was not fooling around. He was in it to win the timed crossing – anything in the forty-day range would do

— and to break a record he and his crews had never crushed despite a number of attempts. We were all completely on board for this victory. We could taste it.

THE *BRITANNIA III*

When I finally came face to face with the *Brittania III*, I could barely take it in. How could this torpedo of a vessel be so long—twenty-eight feet—and yet so compact? Let me try to describe it. Let's start with the cabins.

Painted crimson and snow, the bow cabin (designated the women's cabin) was nothing but a fiberglass/neoprene/Kevlar capsule, with a footwell extending beneath the decks for the rower who would have to sleep there. It looked like a coffin, and it was called that. The footwell was bookended by two three-foot-wide sleeping benches meeting at the point of the "A." There was even a triangular bench for a fourth sleeper to curl up on at the top of the A, if one wrapped oneself around the tube in the middle of it. No room, really, to sit up. A skinny-person-sized hatch opened onto the deck. We would have to try hard to keep this hatch closed to keep our living quarters—and all our stuff—from being deluged by waves. No problem, right?

A wind generator and solar panels adorned the bow cabin roof.

Though larger, the "men's cabin" at the stern was even more suffocating. I was stunned by the amount of equipment in there, including the radio, batteries for the wind generator and for storage of the cabin-top solar battery, GPS, ePIRB (locator beacon), automatic pilot, and water purifier.

Deafening. Even the steering column from the automatic pilot to the rudder went through their cabin. They would have to sleep on two long benches along the sides or the middle bench and one crisscross to make an H of the sleeping bunks. The whole scene was a tangled web of equipment, gear, "beds," and sprawling men. Unlike us, they had two hatches, one at the stern for escape–hmm–and the other out to the rowing platform.

Ah, the rowing platform. Totally surreal.

For those who haven't (yet) had the pleasure of rowing a boat like this, a little tutorial. In our boat, there were four rows of two seats each. The seats were hard and wooden, butt-shaped. Each rower holds one oar. The crew rows "backwards," that is, facing the coxswain – or cox – and a wall festooned with mileage, distance per hour, and automatic pilot info.

The cox, responsible for steering and giving directions, sits in the stern facing the rowers and the course ahead.

The oar pair closest to the coxswain is the stroke pair. They set the pace and keep the stroke rate even and consistent. Everyone else is expected to synchronize with the stroke pair. When they don't, it can get ugly.

The seats slide. Rowers plant their feet in "foot stretchers" and push for every stroke, thrusting hard with their legs for the drive. The idea is to draw yourself up the slide until the knees are at ninety degrees, then propel off the footboards with the force of your quads and core. Rowing is all about legs and core. It is not like a rowboat. It's not really an "arm" sport, as arm muscles just aren't big enough to do what's required. Legs, core, back–these are the work force. Arms are management, just connectors attaching you to the oar. Brains? Best to keep them out of it entirely.

Along with fourteen humans, eight sliding seats, the cox bench, and oars, the *Brittania III* needed all kinds of rigging. First of all, since it's always helpful to be constantly reminded of the good possibility of death close at hand, down the center was a grab line running stern to bow. Our survival gear, including two inflatable (we hoped) lifeboats and sea anchors, ran right down the center, separating the rowers.

Lashed under the rigging on both sides were extra oars in case one broke, which apparently oars did (and would) under the onslaught of the waves.

Other gear was bundled in wet bags and stored between the rowers. Underfoot were the Hendersons: round watertight hatches connecting to the belly of the boat where all our food and snacks were stored. Everything was carefully labeled (snack packs, full meals, paper goods, medications, etc.) and efficiently organized. This was the only part of the boat that really *really* needed to stay dry.

DAYS INTO WEEKS

La Gomera was an interesting French Riviera type of place. From what I could tell, there were no poor areas visible to the tourist eye, just a mix of money and middle class. The day we arrived, the whole town celebrated Dia de los Reyes Magos – Three Kings Day or Epiphany – with parades and festivities well into the night.

I've never been a huge partier, and I didn't feel totally comfortable around so many people all the time. How did my teammates have all this energy? Was I actually starting to feel like the old lady, for the first time in my life. Whatever. I knew I would be able to contribute in plenty of other ways if not on the dance floor.

I was eager to get to work. After breakfast (bocadillos of ham tomato and cheese–HA–bread! –In your EAR, paleo!), we got back to work on more oars, scraping and painting and refurbishing footplates. While we worked, we made some decisions. We voted to sleep on yoga mats instead of air mattresses, for example, to save weight and gain speed. And blow-up pillows, we decided, just might save a life. Really, we were all just imagining what our lives might feel like for the next month. The more we shaped the fantasy together, the more confident we all became.

Worries moved to the edges. We wanted this.

We were also getting to know each other in everyone's favorite way—the gossip machine.

I loved getting to know Roger.

Roger: a behemoth at 6'5," twenty-six years a cop in London who once "did things for people." Meaning? Turns out Roger was a bodyguard, enforcer, private investigator type of guy. His job when we met also involved organizing the annual London-to-Paris women's rowing race. He was also on the Ocean Rowing Society Board of Directors. Bald and tough as nails, the guy was hilarious and fascinating, totally entertaining, a big- time adventurer.

I learned a lot from Roger. For one thing, quite a few years earlier, he'd rowed the Atlantic with one other guy. But just at the finish, at the mouth of the bay in Barbados, they were struggling to stay off the rocks and were offered a "pull-away" by the local Coastguard. Ocean rowing forbids the use of any direct support to qualify as an ocean row. Although he had questioned it and had been reassured, ultimately this meant that their entire row, after thousands of grueling miles, had to be invalidated at the very end—no assistance allowed. Absolutely crushing. I wondered if this row, for Roger, offered some sort of redemption.

✦

Quiet: When you are rowing, you don't talk. Rowing is funny that way, since we are essentially staring at the back of each other's heads. It's also really hard work and requires concentration to stay in sync, so that is the rower's main focus. In my current club, Gloucester Gig Rowers, conversation is allowed only in what we call "recreation rows." On "conditioning rows" or "race practices," talking is discouraged because "if you can talk, you are not pulling hard enough. "

Hearing can also be difficult amidst the noise of the sea, the mechanics, the thunk of the oars and the automatic pilot. As a result, the whole exercise can feel as if you're alone with your own thoughts in your own head. This was just the way I liked it, and I'm pretty sure I wasn't the only rower to feel that way.

Our starting point was yet to be determined, which was a bit nerve-wracking. We didn't know whether we'd have to row to Las Canarias to start the race. It was getting harder to wait.

In between work stints on the boat, there was the constant socializing, 24/7, which I was never all that good at.

It didn't take long for all that chitchat to become too much. In fact, the demons were taking over, as they too often did. I was very aware that it was all a projection of my own deni-grating self, an internal battle. My friends at home knew all about it, but I tried not to display any insecurity around these rippling pillars of confidence.

I hated "fattening up." Excessive eating goes against all my eating disordered instincts. I was happy about the shape I was in, and screwing with that was messing with my head. Of course I knew we were going to row it off. I hated feeling sedentary (although we worked hard on the boat) and really hated eating pizza and sandwiches for dinner. My teammates loved to reprimand me for not eating all the sweets that got passed around – these Brits LOVE their Haribos. But I can't I can't I can't.

Simon Chalk: An obviously brilliant boat builder and ei-dolon of ocean rowing. The man knew the sea. By 2015, Simon had rowed across the ocean ten times and was world renowned. He knew how to measure the boat against the rowers and use every feature to maximize efficiency and speed in all conditions. Being a relative dilettante, I felt incredibly lucky to be learning from the master. His ideas and opinions meant a lot to me. He was also a portly drinker and smoker, stubborn and scrutinizing, with a tendency to with-hold information as a way of exerting power. There were a few times when it seemed as if he may have stayed out a little too late and didn't get to the boat until early afternoon. But Simon was our supreme leader on this trip, and his decisions carried all the weight, so we were beholden to him. And at his mercy.

Here's how it went one evening at the Blue Marlin, where Happy Hour often lasted well into the wee hours. We were all just shooting the breeze (again), Kate was trying to be businesslike, I was trying to get some details about, oh you know, when we might be *launching*, and Simon stood up.

"I've put together the rowing line-ups," he declared. "Here are the shifts."

The table shut up immediately. Suddenly no one was drunk.

"Team A, First shift, Ben and Shaun stroke,..."

Ben and Shaun look at each other with a grin.

"...Roger and Jamie, engine room." This must have been a difficult choice, probably designed to compensate for Roger's great size. The two were powerhouses, so it made sense to put them in the power seats between stroke and bow.

"Dan and Nabs–" Oh shit, I thought, two non-rowers. Dan was tall but definitely still learning, and Nabs, "professional adventurer" and fireplug who billed himself as the first Omani to do anything, had never rowed.

"Beth and Suzanne, you're in the bow."

The bow. It felt like a slap in the face. Yes, someone had to sit in the bow. Yes, the bow is a key position, essential for keeping the rhythm and even steering. But sitting there at the bar that night, all I could hear was a conversation I had with my winning crew coach daughter years earlier. My Boulder team was driving to a regatta, and I put her on speaker phone to pick her brain for help in setting positions for the crew.

"Be honest," I asked. "How would you line up this crew for today's race?"

She didn't realize the whole crew was listening. "Okay, so you put your best rowers in stroke, of course, powerhouse in five and six. I would put your worst rowers in three and four and the bow pair."

That unintentionally public conversation, where I was assigned Seat Three, became a standing joke for all at Boulder Community Rowing. But I wasn't ready to be a joke in this group.

I could feel Simon staring long and hard, trying to gauge my reaction. I guess he knew me better than I thought. There was no choice but to swallow the pride and accept, at least overtly. His assignments did make sense.

Internally, I cascaded into self-doubt, my heart and soul running wild. I wasn't good enough for this adventure. Simon obviously didn't like me. He put me literally in the shit seat, right next to the bucket. And it wasn't like Beth was my favorite person, but she was totally bearable. I didn't care at all that she was Mensa (Did we know what that was? she asked). Thirty days, side by side. The worst part was that it was the right choice.

I know, my reaction was totally bitchy. I know it was the best line up, given what Simon knew about our skills and personalities. Did I think I was going to stroke next to Anna (in her twenties) and Jen (who'd already completed an ocean row)? Or Ben or Shaun, both accomplished master strokes? Still, my psyche and heart were flooded with self-recrimination and fear. I knew what he must have been thinking: "You ARE the loser of the boat, the worst rower, the old woman, the "leftover."

Of course, I came around. I told myself to shut up. What choice did I have?

I pulled myself out of my self-created doldrum. By 9:30 that night, I was starting to feel even a little proud. I'd stood my ground emotionally against those runaway demons. By 10:30, though I felt a little like an extra in a play, I decided just to engage and try to learn. Story of my life? Maybe.

5

You Can't Whistle a Symphony

IN LIMBO

The next day, the gang went off to a party in the mountains. I gave myself the luxury of forgoing that. It became clear that my normal way of being, to help and be industrious and do all tasks, was paying off in terms of getting things done, but not in terms of creating relationships.

I didn't want to put myself out there all day, but I also didn't want to be left out. Would I ever grow up? I had made myself invisible. Hopefully, I mused, I'll wake up tomorrow as regular old me…I'll get up and go for a run and get myself back.

On the morning of January 7, our third day in La Gomera, problems started to get personal. That didn't take long. Roger, the other shift captain, seemed initially to enjoy taking charge while Simon and Kate were off doing business in Tenerife. He loomed formidably over the rest of us gathered in the small apartment.

"Crew," he gruffed, "apparently, some people have not paid." Was he being diplomatic?

His eyes scanned the room, but no hints. Was this a deal-breaker? How could anyone get to this point without paying for the trip?

"As you probably know, Kate had until yesterday to gather up all the paperwork allowing the boat to embark." He seemed to be growing more furious by the minute. "That person," here, he closed his eyes, probably to keep from spitting flames at the offender, "who had been scuba diving all day, had not turned in his passport and other paperwork. He promised Kate he would do so, but instead went home to take a nap."

We were all frozen in our seats. Roger's anger was formidable, and whoever this rower was who hadn't paid was a jerk for jeopardizing our trip. Roger went on to describe how late at night a couple days earlier, Kate had been forced to track down this malcontent with the help of another rower. How that slacker had marched in and slammed the unfinished paperwork down on the table, had been rude enough to bring Kate to tears.

Somehow, this reflected poorly on all of us. Evidently, Simon told Kate not to talk to us while he was gone, something about protecting her and her sanity. What about our sanity, I wondered.

The announcement evoked a variety of reactions. I could feel the group's anger and impatience at Simon as well as some measure of annoyance with Roger for bringing it up without providing further information. Was this supposed to be strategic on Simon's part? It felt like poor management and subterfuge. On top of itching with impatience to get started and frustration at not having what we needed to get all the work done, now people were feeling anxious and hurt.

This endeavor was turning into a psychologist's dream –

group dynamics in action.

At least the boat was nearly ready. That day, we worked until 6 p.m., then I went for a great run up the hillside, then a freezing cold swim on the lava beach. Back to the Blue Marlin for drinks and Internet.

We were still planning to go. Everything would be okay. If I said it enough times, it would surely come true, right?

Saturday the 8th

Ooh, that was rough, but Roger's scolding actually may have served as something of a tension release valve. After that, we all had Chinese food together and laughed. It was like the air had cleared, we had been forgiven and we were still a crew.

Finally, after way too much fretting, everyone simmered down and set out to prove, through hard work, that THEY were not the lazy culprit. Even Father-of-the-Year Dan (pompously, but whatever) took command of the food supplies along with Beth.

The rest of us worked at our usual hard pace, sanding and painting the rudder and the two dagger boards, assembling the seats on the wheels. I swear Simon told Shaun, a boat builder and fellow rower (destined to be youngest to row the Atlantic), that if we ran out of jobs, "make the crew sand things." Again. And again.

✦

Shaun: What a sweet, good boy, rowing this trip in honor of his Mum who had cancer, raising money for cancer research. A skinny adolescent lad with tousled curly hair and not the grandest hygiene, Shaun was a hard worker, an excellent rower, and my friend and my confidant. Although his Cockney accent was also almost unintelligible for this American, this kid had more common sense than all of us put together. In the running to set the Guinness "Youngest Rower" record, Shaunie was the only rower who never ever complained. I respected him deeply.

We spent ten hours sorting and vacuum-packing 480 two-person meal packs. In each meal pack: two breakfasts, four main meals, and one pudding for the rowing pair. OMIGOD this was a job. When we ran out of bags, I walked to the big supermarket five miles away to buy new ones, but then, since it was Sunday and the store was closed, I trudged back. We packed up what food we could, but ran out. Did what we could on the boat, but were missing too many important things.

Jen has very much calmed down. Although still an outrageous flirt, she and I are getting along well. We can be very direct with each other in part because it really doesn't matter and because we might as well be. She has been sick with a cold and went to the hospital yesterday as part of a self-admitted "part of the drama in my life." She has a cold, the doctor said. She appears to be a bit of an ally, having bought shampoo/soap for all of us to share on the boat.

Simon was in Tenerife trying to sort out the paperwork. But he was also focused on readying another crew's boat, which turned out to be the real reason we were not leaving. This other crew, Ollie and Serge, had financially supported Woodvale, and now they were looking to row a Woodvale double for a record. Simon, of course, felt obliged to facilitate their race, but he could have planned a little better. Everyone was chafing over the delays, grumbling and angry. Had we known, we could have come to the Canaries later. Instead, we sat and waited. This was distressing.

Sunday Jan. 9

we have nothing to do until Simon gets back. I am pretty annoyed as I would not have come to the Canary Islands early had I known this. I am at a café taking care of finances. Poor Gabby, my adolescent office manager who is paying my bills, made an error that caused quite a bit of chaos. As Mike pointed out, she knows about as much about paying bills as any 15 —year-old who doesn't even have a checking account, so, not her fault. Nevertheless, it was an excellent thing to hang anxiety on, so was up at 3 obsessing about business finances and not being able to do a thing to resolve the problems long distance. This is the first time in my life I have taken any substantial time off from work which makes sense not to do when you work for yourself.

Off to a group rooftop Yoga session this morning taught by Guy's lovely daughter Saskia. Guy's wife Debs and his daughter Saskia are here to see Guy off and have been instrumental in the preparation process.

Yoga makes me want to laugh — I love the exercise part of it but I hate the meditation part (which is probably what I need the most but which makes me so feverishly impatient). I will be lying there trying frantically to "be one with my breathing" and "listen just to my breathing and quiet my mind" and the whole time my body and mind are screaming "do something, you have

so much to do, stop lying around here like a big flat X
on the ground and get to it" – clearly I am not a good
meditator. However, we did realize how horribly stiff
and sore we all were from the outrageous positions we
must bend ourselves into to accommodate the cramped
corners and pockets of Brittannia.

Guy: Straight-up summertime. Brought up in East Africa
speaking Swahili then moving to Wales, he was sure of himself and refreshingly confident without having to diminish
anyone else. Guy was involved with a company called BNI
and had set up a number of chapters around the UK. His
wife, Debs, who was there for his departure, pointed out
that Guy was a champion swimmer, which you could believe
judging from his Tarzan physique. He was rowing for his
father, who instilled in him a love of the sea, but who was
killed too soon, before they were able to share enough of it
together. He could even get tearful about his father. Guy
was the "grown up" amongst us. We all loved him.

When Simon finally came back, he wouldn't speak to us.
This was kind of a magical relief. First of all, I didn't have it
wrong: he didn't like me. But he didn't like anyone. He was,
I decided, actually pretty narcissistic and immature. He sent
Roger in his stead to announce we had nothing more to do
on the boats. The rest was for the professionals. Go away. We
will let you know if we want you. Be ready to leave next week.

Our Brits surprised me with a sort of peppy acquiescence.
They got all excited about a dumb costume party, something
that was supposed to mollify the crew, but which only pissed
me off. Horrors, dressing up? It made me want to go to sleep
immediately.

Boat wasn't ready. Food wasn't ready. There was nothing
we could do.

> **The British** among us were VERY different as a whole, with a kind of fatalism that seemed both calming to them personally and easier on others. The Brits could shut down completely and immediately or, alternatively, slide into cheerful acceptance. There was certainly no room for any kind of expression of anger. Do North Americans have more heart attacks? Maybe we have fewer.

OMMM...

Jan 12th

Wrote a note to my daughter, "I am sharing my M&Ms for breakfast."

Simon weighed our bags to make sure we were under the limit. That required my jettisoning some of my own things such as personal supplies of Ibuprofen, etc. We were allowed shared toothpaste only, among other toiletries and gear. Jen swore she had enough shampoo and toothpaste for all of us.

After weighing my bag, Simon restored himself somewhat as a human being. He must have made a conscious decision to answer me when I spoke to him. Phew, it would have been a long thirty days. He shared the story of his two-year-old son sustaining getting injured in a terrible accident. The child, miraculously, survived the ordeal unscathed, but his dad–maybe not so much. I wondered if this could explain a bit of Simon's psyche.

Meanwhile, Dan and Beth had become an item. Sort of a perfect couple: Beth appeared to be desperate, and Dan was desperately horny. Oh well. Interesting to watch.

> **Dan** was a boatload of contradictions. He rowed to his own beat, but was also, for the most part, steadfast. Both a sexist and a pain in the butt, he was also a good mate with some interesting personality quirks. He could be nasty one minute, incredibly generous the next. I'll always be grateful to Dan for planting this Woodvale seed in my head and heart.

I was happy to head off to yoga. Get my om on.

WE ROW

Finally! We got the boat in the water at great peril to all involved. The harbor had inadequate equipment to sling the boat up out of the trailer and into the water, so Simon's compromise was to put all of the men in the stern of the boat, weighing it down. The bow tipped and stayed up even though the sling was not mid-ships, an upended torpedo lowered into the water. The guys, imagining the boat slipping from the sling and smashing to the concrete below, predicted that this experience might count as one of the scariest events of the entire Atlantic voyage. But we were launched!

Rowing again! Omigod, it was something. The boat was quite light, even though it was packed with our food as ballast. The trim depended completely on where people were sitting and had to be modified at all times. It was HARD. Of course, I was wearing flip-flops and my feet kept falling out of the foot stretchers.

We weren't supposed to be feathering. Feathering required sliding back to the catch position with the oar blades horizontal to the water to minimize drag. On a three-thousand-mile trip, flipping the oar would cause terrible wear and tear on our wrists. Also, we had to take much shorter strokes than we were used to because, with so many people in that short space, the foot stretchers had to be closer to the seat, putting extra strain on the legs.

That first day of rowing was, not surprisingly, a fiasco. No one kept any kind of rhythm, and I'm sure I'm not the only one whose kidneys ached from being bashed by the oars behind us. We'd figure it out, right?

And the rumors were true: the poop bucket would, in fact, be right between Beth and me. Everyone was very self-conscious about having to use the bathroom so...publicly. The bucket was also right in front of our cabin door, so our view would be someone's buttocks, and our fresh ocean air..., not so fresh. Oh boy. It was a very small boat.

Fourteen people crawling around, going about their business, would be quite a trick. On the flip side, my onboard travels would be limited to the journey from seat to cabin, which happened to be right next to each other. You couldn't walk or stand in the boat as you'd immediately be pitched overboard, so crawling over the bags amidships (parachute anchors, lifeboats, etc.) was difficult and painful on the knees. The center line for stability swayed so much that it could never be depended upon. It quickly became very clear what a marvelous and amazing challenge this would be. Right?

After the row, a meeting.

"My expectations are that you all take this race very seriously," Simon began. "I want to break the record, and that means rowing this bloody ocean in thirty-three days." He scanned the group, still seeming to be assessing each one of us and our worthiness. "And don't forget. Each of you is allowed twenty pounds of gear total, including your foulies." I always loved being berated in advance of any wrongdoing. But whatever.

"One last thing," he continued, grave and intense. "Before you all disperse, I have an important issue to clarify: nudity." A few chuckles. Maybe a groan.

"Don't worry," I jumped in. "This is not an issue for the women. We are well aware that the men often row nude."

Simon took a deep breath. "No, Suzanne. This is about female nudity. One of the crew's wives called me with a serious issue. She's demanding that you women may not row in the nude."

The four of us women almost laughed aloud.

At least he looked a little embarrassed. I hadn't seen that before. "If you women don't agree, she's told us, her husband cannot go."

You'd think we'd mutiny right then and there, right? You'd think we'd balk at the injustice, the ridiculous sexism, the outrageous demand coming from someone who wasn't even part of the team. We didn't.

"Looks like we will have to accept it," we agreed. Honestly, we probably wouldn't have rowed nude anyway. The idea was irksome, different rules for different genders, but whatever. "Guess we have to tolerate – or is it celebrate? – male nudity!" When did I get so agreeable? I just wanted to row. Let's go, people.

Later that day, we were advised the Spanish authorities had refused to allow us to embark from La Gomera. We would have to move the boat nearly two hundred miles, an eight-hour drive including a ferry ride, to Porto Mogan in La Canaria. Time was running out.

LA CANARIA

Jan 13th

Most unfortunately, we had to drive the boat to our starting point in La Canaria. Roger, Jamie, and I were elected to go with the boat while the rest of the team stayed behind to finish packing up the food. Traveling with the boat on a trailer is a trip in itself, especially since Roger drives either too carelessly or like an old lady.

Jamie was tall and shaggy, hearty and kind, tousled brown hair and warm brown eyes. He seemed like the type who would be an engaged and fun father and stalwart crewmate. He was so mellow, always fairly accepting (to me) of what was happening, but also SO anxious about running out of time. He and Colin had a verbal dance going that often left me weak with laughter.

Colin, lovely Colin. Handsome and self-effacing, transparent and open. A gentleman, so bright and sweet and kind. Colin was an elegant *and* hilarious young man with a girlfriend. He worked as an event planner for Buckingham Palace. He was clearly a rower, adding enormous value to the team and 100% committed to the task.

We got to know each other over drinks.

"Where are you from?" Everyone's starting off point for every conversation.

"Colorado, and you?"

"I'm from South Africa," Jamie grinned (ruefully?). "That is where my wife is now, and we have a new baby."

"Oh man, congratulations!" I patted his shoulder. "It must be hard to be away from them."

"Yeah, it is." He took a long swallow. "I'm actually feeling a little frantic. I promised work and family I'd be back before March. Looks like I'm going to run out of time." His eyes were pained, crestfallen. This adventure was clearly a life's dream for him.

We discussed apartheid in South Africa and what it meant for him to grow up in a world of black people. How shocked he was by racism when he moved away from South Africa. When his father died, his mother found a job at the mine, brought up her two boys on her own, then sent them to boarding school thanks to the mining company.

We finally arrived at the ferry dock at La Gomera. Roger was at it again, careless at the wheel. We were just trying to find the exit when he swung the back of the trailer and the boat into a cement wall. No No No!!! There was a very large hole in the boat, in the keel. Finding Kevlar and fiberglass on a Sunday evening was impossible. We tried really hard, though, knowing that the alternative would be ugly. And it was.

Roger called Simon to confess. Simon thought we were joking – haha. But when the truth dawned on him, you could hear him swearing over the phone, shouting. But he promised to take care of it, to send his boatbuilding boys to us as soon as he could. Another crisis averted. Maybe.

Late that night, we were detained at the border in La Canaria, accused of importing a boat. The UK guys were furious as the Canary Islands were part of Spain and thus in the EU, and didn't they have the right to go anywhere they pleased? They were being a bit confrontational. It required some fancy Spanish speaking on my part to convince them to let us go.

We were supposed to stop halfway and bunk ourselves on the side of the road in either the boat or the car, but we decided it was silly and we might as well keep going. Finally, we pulled into Porto Mogan very late and a bit rattled, ready to get rowing.

6

Lose Some, Win Some

NOT MUTINY

Jan. 14

Trenzas are a go mañana. One of the big concerns for all of us is not being able to bathe and the condition of our hair. Anna and I decided we would have our hair braided a la Bo Derek. Oh my, as it turns out this is not a good look, especially for an older woman. Anna looks pretty cute, though. Bo Derek we are not. I can only hope my braids fall out soon. Everyone was polite enough not to laugh uproariously. I immediately donned my rowing cap which I will keep on always.

The hostel is a lovely place. Andrea has renovated it herself with the type of bright and unique funkiness I love. We have a woman's "dorm" with bunk beds.

Two men's dorms. There are another four people living
on the roof — 2 young German women who do the
cleaning in exchange for bunks and an Icelandic fellow and his boyfriend and a kind of mean and smelly
"manager."

The rest of the crew arrived over the weekend, but no Simon.
That meant another "day off." No one wanted a day off. We
wanted to get out of there and row. Maybe this was a test for
us all. Another one. At least Simon's boat builders had arrived
and were focused on repairing the boat. They were magicians.

Still, Sunday evening, the shit kind of hit the fan. Dan was
furious about all of the delays.

"I think we need a new captain," he steamed. "I think we
need to fire Simon and insist on someone else taking us. He is
so much more focused on the other boat and so disorganized
about getting us out that we are wasting time."

In spite of his insistence that we leap to action, we were
shocked into uncomfortable silence. It was not that we dis-
agreed with his beef, but Simon *was* Woodvale. He built the
boat, he was the most competent captain, and if not Simon,
who? This would be mutiny.

It didn't take long after that for Simon to show up. Dear
Lord. He knew about Dan trying to inveigle us all to hire a
new skipper and essentially attempting to wreak dissension.
Simon called Dan out, labeled him an asshole for rabble rous-
ing behind his back, accused him of not being a man. In fact,
Simon had a massive temper tantrum, once again proving that
the best defense was a good offense.

"This ain't no pansy ass bullshit Atlantic crossing," he
seethed. "People, we are in it to break the record." He also
pointed out that he was well aware that there were a handful
of folks doing all the work. Thankfully, my own neuroses lend
themselves furiously to being one of the worker-bees. And

phew. I would not have liked to have been at the receiving end of THAT tirade.

Things got worrisome when the couple of rowers he singled out to reprimand erupted in protest, whining and lying outright to cover their asses. Simon was irate and called Dan a liar. Which he was. I couldn't tell if Dan was going to break down or explode. You could almost see the gears spinning out of control in his big head.

After he'd bent everyone to his will and regained control, Simon admitted he was not the best people manager, then softened on everything and gave us a much-needed pep talk. He reminded us that this was not just a row across the Atlantic—anyone could do that. This race was a serious world record attempt, and "If you are not in," he growled, "you are out."

Eventually, all were appropriately chastened and, more importantly, available to help put the boat in the water.

THE RECRUIT

Jamie had to leave. As predicted, he had run out of time and had to say goodbye, kissing us all tearfully and taking his leave. We were horrified. There was a tremendous hole left by his absence as he was not just a very good guy, but also a leader within the group. What a shame to have put in so much money and time, only to have to give it all up because we were not leaving as promised.

Suddenly we were in something of a pickle. Did anyone know anyone who was looking for a gigantic adventure? Who wanted to join this crew essentially with their boat passage paid for? I asked my daughter to use her rowing connections, so she sent out an email to Riverside Rowing Club in Boston, and within thirty minutes it had spread across the rowing world.

As a result, Jonathon.

Jonathon (in his own words):
"Here is why I am qualified for this challenge:
- Belmont Hill School (1986-1989)
- Dartmouth Heavyweight Crew 1992
- Great Eight (Voted Top US Men's Collegiate Heavyweight Crew)
- #1 Eastern Sprints; #1 IRAs; #2 (by 2") Nationals
- Henley Royal Regatta 1992
- Silver Medal - Head of the Charles Alumni Event 2010

Our 1992 "Great Eight" boat competed in the 2010 Head of the Charles. We (18 years later) matched our college rowing weights and exceeded our college rowing fitness. The week following the Head I pulled an 8606m 30 min piece (1:44.5 splits). I am fit."

Jonathon (my words) was tall, gangly, long necked, and loping, something of a narcissist. When he broke an oar, he dubbed himself "Oar Breaker." He had been living in Japan with his lawyer Canadian/Japanese wife, and had two babies, one of whom he'd never actually met since he'd moved to the Caribbean where he was studying for his sea captain's license. I tried to connect with him, but, in my eyes, he was mostly about his own specialness.

MORE ABOUT THE BOAT

The good part was the rowing, training on the water. First of all, I was grateful every day to husband Mike, whose five thousand-song playlist kept my brain awake and alive, even though it was mostly country-western. It was also pretty inspiring to notice all the work we had done on the boat. We'd sanded the oars and painted them crimson, checked the foot stretchers, loaded the Hendersons, affixed the yoga mats to the benches, and packed the deck with equipment.

One of many astonishing things about an open small boat like the *Brittania III* was that every last item had to be tied down, including the oars. Everything. Cups, seats, even the humans were attached to the boat by a surfer's leash which, in my eyes, was a placebo. If the boat were to roll over, the leash would just break and we would be 100% out of luck unless we could somehow manage to hold on for dear life. During shift changes—probably the most dangerous activity we performed—we'd have to detach from the leash and teeter unfettered from seat to cabin holding onto a line that stretched from stem to stern. I had no confidence in the system, but whatever. We weren't going to roll over, right? (Not surprisingly, these lines were jettisoned after the first day when their uselessness became apparent).

The infamous poop bucket sat right in front of our cabin hatch. Nice. We hung a silk curtain to provide a modicum of privacy, to help us avoid having to stare at the buttocks of those using the loo, and to prevent the pestilent odors from wafting in.

It wasn't all bad, of course. The lucky thing about being in a bow seat, we discovered, was that we could enjoy relative security, privacy, and safety while doing our business by putting the bucket right in our own footwell. This method became fashionable pretty quick. As the shift arrangements changed, the bucket was passed like a cup of tea to the person in need to allow them to crouch in their footwell and do their business. It was then up to the user to tie the bucket to the rigging and clean it in the ocean waves.

But the actual rowing. The cliffs of Porto Mogan were stunning and exciting, almost like a movie set. Moving our bodies and our boat through the clear azure waves, the cliffs rising behind us—just wow. None of us was in it for the scenery, but no one could deny that feeling of awe.

STILL WAITING

Friday Jan. 21

At the hostel. The short bald Icelandic guy, taken to affectations such as an Alpine hat (even indoors), checkered pants and a pipe, just walked by making grating noises. He sounded like an old car trying to start in winter. I asked him if he were talking to himself and he said no, he was trying to sing but that it took his voice a long time to start up in the morning. Especially after too much whisky. HA.

Driving rain all day. Huge waves. So glad we were not out there.

When we weren't rowing, we spent a lot of time at the bar. There was so much to discuss, to imagine, to plan for, and to celebrate. When Simon's son, Ollie, turned three, well, what were we going to do? All of us loved spending time with this kid, and the adoration was mutual.

One day, a bunch of us were crossing the street. Suddenly, little Ollie darted out into the oncoming traffic and, before anyone could even respond other than to gasp in horror, Shaun grabbed the toddler's shoulder and, with great equanimity, re-directed him back to safety, clearly saving the child's life. Shaunie was humble about it, barely seeming to recognize how he had just saved a child from being bludgeoned by a car. That was Shaun. That was how our days were going as the waiting stretched on.

Jan 21 (cont.)

At about 10:00 p.m. leaving the bar, we were sought out by a deranged blonde woman reporting that our boat was bashing itself against the boats next to it, destroying itself and the adjoining boats. Daring night-time boat rescue!!! Now, the word is the crazy lady is one of the best women skippers on the Atlantic but is also an infamous con artist bilking tourists out of thousands. Her boat has been impounded and she lives on a rental. However, in this moment she did help us.

Against buffeting wind and waves we moved the boat across the harbor. It was scary and exciting and again confirmed why we are SO glad we are not out in the sea at the moment. The bashing broke three oar locks. The leaks previously discovered are being repaired to-day. 3:00 am the tide went out so the anchor line rubbed a good bit of paint and fiberglass off the stern of the boat. Jeez.

AT THE BAR

Nabs comported himself like a prince, and so we thought of him that way. Born in London but definitely a citizen of the world, he was able and self-assured without being dominating. Elegant, well-educated, and confident, Nabs' life involved one terrific adventure after another – mountain climbing, scuba diving, trekking to the magnetic North Pole – and he claimed to be the first Arab ever to row an ocean.

Things were getting out of hand at the bar. Swarthy and

strong, Nabs was quite the favorite with some of the French women. For reasons that escaped the rest of us, les femmes took it upon themselves to accost us women, angrily accusing us of being responsible in advance for the eventual death of the men in our boat.

"Murder," they cried. "You women, you vil kill dem. You should not be on ze boat at all!"

"Pas du tout! Get off this crew now!" another one shrieked.

"Just sink of zese poor gorgeous men." She batted her eyelashes at Nabs.

We were laughing. "What are you talking about?"

"You women," snarled the one with the bright red bob and the longest fingernails I'd ever seen, "you vill be having blood." She broadly indicated the area of her uterus and below. "Avoir ses regles! Ze blood, ze smell, it will, what do you say, attract les requins! Ze sharks!"

"Zey vill gnash ze men to death." The blonde's eyes were so big, I worried they could pop out any moment.

They really seemed to believe it, that our menstruation would attract sharks, who would promptly go into a frenzy and tear the poor gorgeous men to shreds. (That they'd probably chow on the women, too, did not seem to cause much concern.)

As their voices got higher and higher, we scurried away.

It was all pretty funny, except that most of the women (present menopausal company excepted) were actually seriously worried about what to do at that time of the month. I mean, you know. Somehow it felt like that was a part of our plumbing that would have to be kept secret for some reason—maximum discretion required. Why? Not sure. There was also a good chance that the stress of overexercise and poor nutrition could bring on amenorrhea, so...that would solve the shark problem.

Jan. 22

Today Roger told us a story about another rower, Bobby. He's about to make his 3rd attempt at the record.
1st one, they were blown to Cape Verde. 2nd attempt,
he and his partner hit high seas and the boat rolled and
didn't self-right. They had to abandon ship to a life
raft that got punctured in the escape and started to
sink. Their general E-PIRB (locator device) broke, and
they only had a small one that gave a beacon for planes
flying overhead.

They were at sea for 48 forty eight hours in a sinking life raft when a yacht picked them up. The yacht
owners refused to allow them to go below deck, nor
would they give them food, clothing or water. When
Bobby and Colin insisted on being given care according to maritime law, the yacht people FORCED THEM
OFF THE BOAT AT GUNPOINT BACK INTO THE
SINKING LIFE RAFT.

Holy shit, can you imagine their despair? Clearly it was
a drug yacht or human trafficking or some such thing.
So these boys were back in a sinking life raft 3 hours
before a passing plane heard the beacon and sent another yacht to rescue.

Anyway, what a story. It won't be us.

HOMESICK

Thursday Jan. 26

I miss everyone so much. Not whining or complaining!

Indeed who could be luckier in life than I? However, as I had kind of expected, it is somewhat difficult to be the mom/grandma here. Just a different life and a different lifestyle that is, after all, perfectly okay but leaves me yearning for my compadres (or madres) to spend time with.

I feel like I'm just "there." Lying in bed this morning, I reminded myself again to not attribute meanings to other people's behavior. Just old paranoia about being liked when there is no reason to believe I am not. I just make stuff up. Silly. Every day I contemplate if I should leave and go back to the US. I miss them all, my family, more each day and send them love.

Today we were shooed away from the boat to let the boat builders finish repairs. We are really (supposedly) leaving Sunday. Maybe Sunday night. There is no doubt but these are the most optimal conditions and we could break the record.

Group gossip: Beth relinquished her relationship with Dan and latched onto Jonathan the Mighty Oar Breaker. They are very well designed for each other in their dizzy goofiness.

Jonathan wasn't turning out to be as much of a dud as I had thought. He'd had a career in finance, got divorced, and left all to find his dream on the sea. I mean, at least he had a job at some point.

Beth would sit at his feet, stroking his leg. Kinda made me nauseated and uncomfortable, the overt possessiveness and neediness of it all. First Dan, now Jonathan. The ickiest part was that he wasn't really reciprocating, instead pretty much ignoring her. But she was relentless. So lonely. And I sorta understood why.

✦

Simon was really excited and, after all of his ocean rows, he clearly felt the record was now within his grasp. Our grasp. We were looking at thirty-forty-foot swells the whole way and at least eighteen-knot winds at our back – maybe up to twenty-five knots. The brutal weather was supposed to diminish after several days, but oh boy. It was getting really real. I like that Simon felt good about us as a crew. I was crossing my fingers.

I was also terrified and not looking forward to that first week of vomiting. We had canned peaches for the first three days – two cans each, because canned fruit, according to Simon, "tastes the same going down as coming back up." Dear Lord.

LAST DAY

Jan 28

Over time, we all evolve to ourselves. I am used to being alone, so I am often alone. Not much of a joiner. I prefer home, family, friends, routine, my stuff, and my life. I also love adventure and travel, seeing new things and being active.

Colin had a really good idea for his journal. He's come up with a series of questions to answer daily, prompts to examine his mood, what he'd contributed that day, and what he took away from, or cost, the boat. I like that idea. Maybe I'll try it out, too.

Roy, a neighbor rower and boat builder, threw a BBQ for us that Friday night so people could have one last night of drinking without fear of the impact on the boat. These people ate more than anything I had ever seen. And drank. I was a total lightweight, and teased without mercy because I really only drink Pinot Grigio.

We were all getting along pretty well. I guess I should stop worrying, I told myself. HA.

After the barbecue, I sat on a rooftop and gazed at a murmuration of white-grey birds wheeling around and around the house. They blanketed the sky, and the whir of their wings created a little breeze.

We learned at the morning meeting that we'd be leaving Sunday. We needed permission to go. No one else spoke Spanish, so I trotted over to the harbormaster at the archaic port authority building to get all the papers signed and "el permiso" to leave port. Did it early just in case there were any snafus. We were good. Did some laundry.

Saturday would be quiet. We'd repack the boat and get really truly ready to go.

I notified my family and friends, promising (again) to send plenty of photos. Otherwise, they'd never believe me. Mostly they would never believe that I could wear the same outfits every day, hair noticeably greying, no color on my nails. I already looked like a beach scavenger woman, and we hadn't even left yet.

ACTUAL LAST DAY

Saturday. While I was working on the boat, talking to all of the tourists, I met this interesting American, Pierre Honegger, former *Time Magazine* foreign correspondent, possessor of a fleet of race cars, and owner of La Voile French restaurant in Boston (amongst others). He invited me to join him for dinner on his yacht, *Aldebaran*. I brought a bottle of wine down to his gorgeous South American teak sailboat. We had a delightful evening, particularly since our politics are so similar. What fun. And what a stunning yacht.

When I came back from my special evening, everyone in the hostel gathered to say goodbye to us, a festive farewell. The guest from Iceland, Egzeus, wrote us a song.

The rowers are getting ready
For their journey out to sea
The bucket has been emptied
For all of them to pee.
The boat is sitting pretty
It gleams in the mid-day sun
This trip will be a big adventure
I'm sure you'll all have fun
You've waited very patiently
Some may say too long
It's easy to dwindle the hours away
Just get Roger to sing a song.
Egzeus will soothe your worries
With a quick rub on your back
Please remain conscious
Or he may want to rub your crack.
The moral of this poem
Is to wish you the best of luck
You're gonna break the record
Because all the others suck!

News flash: they lied, we were not leaving Sunday.

FINALLY

Monday, January 31

In spite of everything, our departure was delayed till

close to 1:00 p.m., much to my everlasting impatience. At least it gives me a few minutes to write.

The morning did not start fortuitously — at the hostel we were out on the deck and heard a huge crash and a man screaming and trying to get from his balcony back into the apartment (elderly German couple). Fearing an incident of domestic violence, Mike the fireman/ EMT and I (the translator) ran over. As it turned out, the woman had had a heart attack and died wedged against the French door from the inside, with one arm thrust through the glass. Mike had to do CPR until the emergency people came — even finding the ER number required my running up and down the walkways asking neighbors. It was sad and depressing. Some vacation for them. I believed she died···how horrible.

Life is fragile.

Embarking on this boat adventure meant we had to leave the land adventure. We brought up a broken oar to give to Andrea, our landlady, as a gift. She was so proud.

All of our extra baggage was loaded into the vehicles headed back to Great Britain. I had my computer and clothing and all things of daily living, but Anna's parents were kind enough to offer to bring it all with them to Barbados. I knew I could trust them with my wallet and the mementos I'd found down here: a hanging string of candles, a gecko hook, a wall decoration gecko.

My ten-pound kit for the race consisted of two pairs of running shorts, a bathing suit, two t-shirts (wool), two pairs of wool socks (Smartwool we love you so), my Crocs, a lightweight rain jacket from REI, a water bottle, my electric toothbrush and paste (okay, I was obsessed with tooth brushing and the charge would last the month), a hair brush, Regan's waterproof book of photos, notebooks, waterproof pens, some chewing gum, the pillow, and my foul weather gear. I also had an extra pair of cheap sneakers I'd picked up on a whim, and one set of earphones, two iPods—one with books to listen to and the other with Mike's music collection. Around my neck dangled Andrew's St. Christopher medal to assure a safe return home.

Not a lot of gear for thirty-three days.

Our watch (Team A) rowed out of the harbor to much fanfare, cheers and shouts and wild applause. Everyone was out on the docks cheering an enormous HURRAH, and people honked wildly from their own boats. It was pretty exciting. No, exalting. We left under conditions Big Spirit had promised us would shoot us straight to a record-breaking win.

The Woodvale Challenge

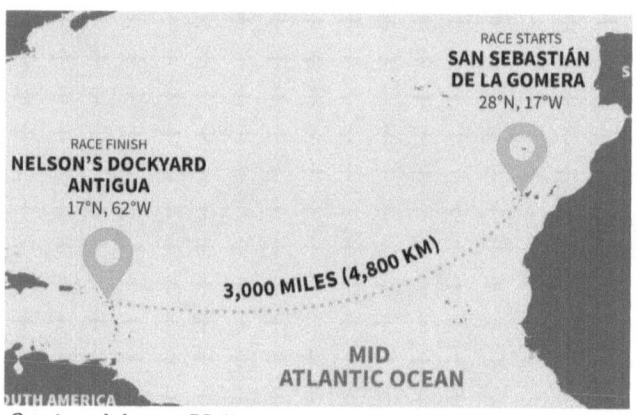

Our intended route (HA)

Suzanne in training

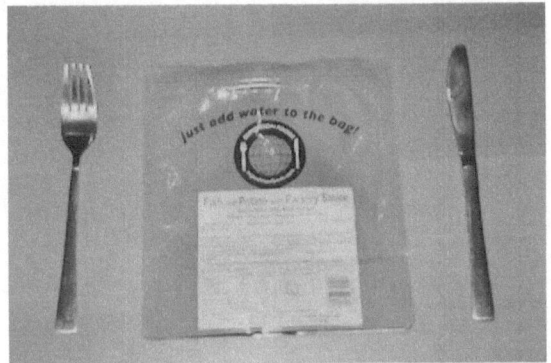

Breakfast, lunch, and dinner

The world's toughest rowboat

We row!

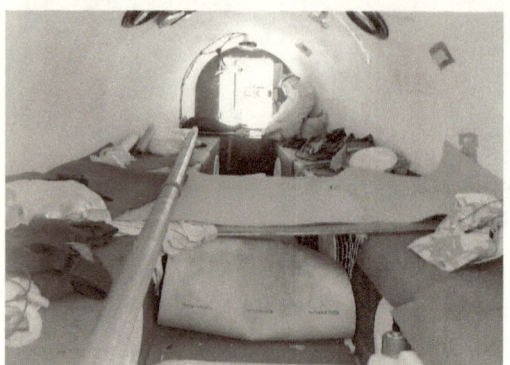

The men's cabin

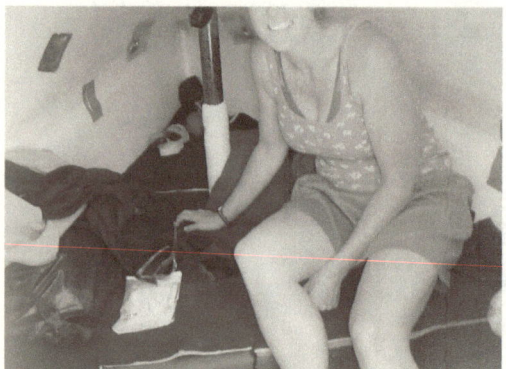

The women's cabin

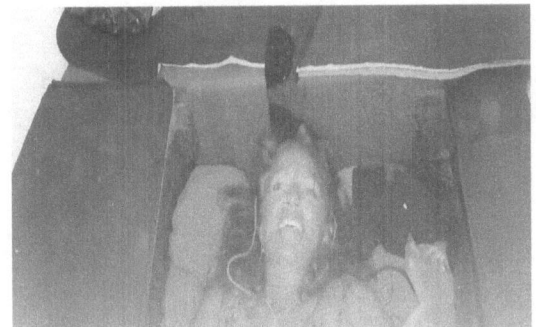

The despised and dreaded coffin

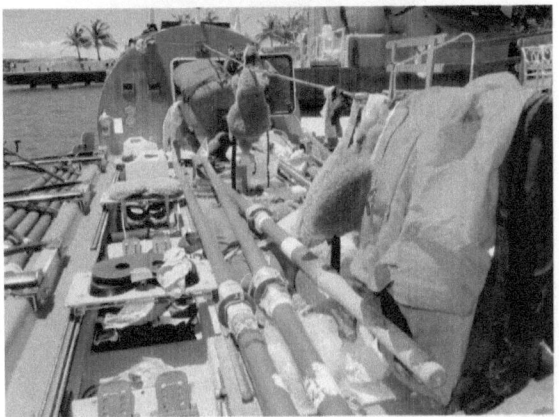

The walk of the dead monkeys

Hard at work

Cabin wall birthday joy

Infamous cock sock

Remodeled toilet facilities

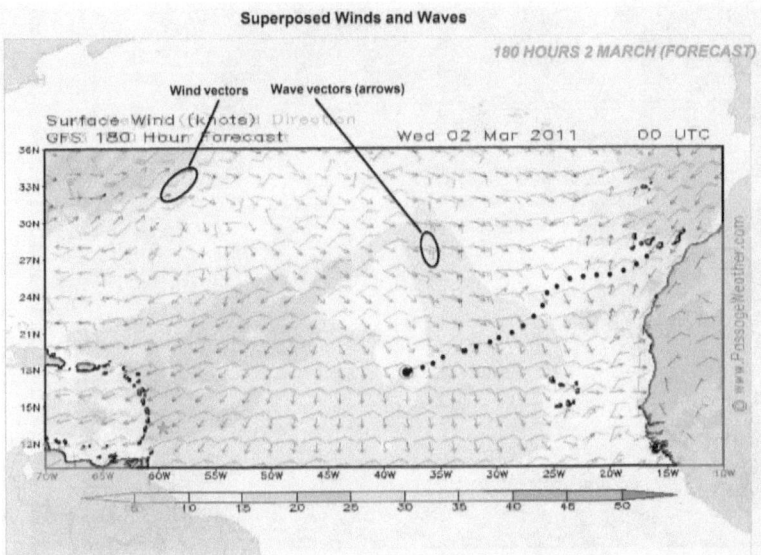

The winds and waves weren't always with us

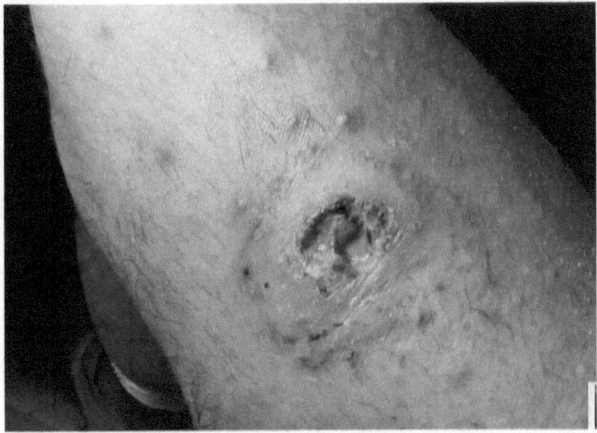

MRSA destroys our bodies

Land HO!

All smiles - Back row: Jonathan, Captain Mike, Shaun, Roger, Ben
Middle row: Dan, Guy, Nabs, Captain Simon, Colin
Front row: Beth, Anna, Suzanne, Jen

PART THREE

During

7

Week One

Bitter Blisters and Brutal Waves

Our jubilation lasted about three hours. In fact, by the end of the first day, we were soaked and freezing, battered and afraid.

Just brutal. Huge walls of water were constantly cascading over the boat. The waves grabbed the oars and smacked them hard against our bodies, especially the shins. Everyone was horribly seasick. The sheets of water made it feel as you were rowing blind. From a misty last look at the cliffs of La Gomera, we were quickly swallowed into the maelstrom of the sea and conditions. And it was very very cold.

We'd been told that purchasing foulies—foul weather gear, the slick and ungainly waterproof hooded jackets and overalls boasting heavy-duty construction that allegedly could withstand whatever punishment the marine environment meted out—was optional. Within the first 24 hours, we realized that foulies were definitely not optional, and not necessarily just for outside. The company had said nothing about sleeping in them, but we discovered that after crawling into the cabin too exhausted to undress, our dripping foulies were just as good as Mama's pajamas.

After our first shift, we tried to sleep in the bucking, soaking cabin, wrapped up in our foulies and trying not to get slammed against the cabin wall. No fan of the cold, my teeth were chattering. Even after only one shift, my muscles ached from the battle with the oars and the sea.

I was also terrified. Just being on the deck was a nightmare. Try to crawl from the seat to the cabin, you took your life in your hands. 26-mph winds and 30-40 ft. swells meant that if a person were to be swept off the boat, we would never be able to turn around and get back to them. The best we could do would be to throw out a life preserver and maybe, if there was time, a lifeboat. But the sea was running by so fast. We'd never find the life preserver or the lifeboat...or the human.

Day 1, Feb 1

It is difficult to write. After a month of journaling in a cozy bedroom or on a sunny deck, crawling into this smelly, soaked cabin to write and sleep between rowing shifts is a shock. I try to hang on to my hard, unforgiving, yoga mat-covered sleeping bench. I have to struggle to not fall into the footwell with each toss of the boat. I feel nauseous and it is causing a headache.

I need my flashlight to write in the gloom, but I am grateful for the waterproof journal and diver's pen as a fat bead of water from the hood of my foul

weather gear plops on the page along with the droplets
dribbling from the ceiling. I look around and there is
no place to hang my foulies to dry so I might as well
crouch (and will sleep) on the dry side of the neo-
prene overalls and jacket. It is cold. My pen is skittering
across the page with the constant smack of the waves
against the rolling boat. The unanimous thunk of oars
hitting oarlocks with each stroke is hypnotic and I am
so exhausted I just want to sleep.

I made a promise to myself to write something every
rest shift. So far so good.

Team A: Roger, Ben, Shaun, Beth, Jonathan, Suzanne and Dan
Team B: Simon, Mike, Anna, Colin, Nabs, Jen, and Guy

There were fourteen of us on board, six rowers and one coxswain per shift. At first, we abided by Anna's creative schedule. The idea was that each person would row for four hours,
then take a one-hour break, rotating through the rowing seats
so each would row in each position. At first, rowing for four
hours straight was no big deal. Right? Anybody can row for
four hours.

We thought the staggering would work. It didn't. With so
many intricate changes in our movements, it was dangerous to
move about and switch seats. We decided each team would do
two two-hour shifts (also called watches) every morning. In
the afternoons, each team would do two three-hour shifts and,
at night, four hours each.

The cox monitored the SAT phone, GPS, and the automatic pilot and took charge of cooking duties. Cooking meant
boiling water on solid fuel sternos and mixing it into the
pouches of dehydrated camping food, then filling our water
bottles using the desalinator. They were also tasked with hand-

ing out the snack packs (candy, dried fruit and nuts) and Pero-nin (hot chocolate!) at night.

During breaks, the most important thing to do was rest, recover, and eat. There was always all kinds of work to do: readjust our stretchers, secure all lines, get drinking water, and eat.

On our off shifts, we were essentially sleepless or besieged by survival nightmares. Fear of drowning permeated our souls and led to fitful rest. The four hours of REM sleep neces-sary to recharge our batteries was impossible to achieve. Sleep deprivation quickly and incredibly turned into hallucinations during rowing shifts. It might have been funny if it hadn't been so freaky.

Our cabin: Hotel California – such a lovely place. "Plenty of room at the Hotel California." It became our theme song. The women's cabin was a seven-foot-long bullet in the bow that included a well below decks, "the coffin." We knew to ex-pect inadequate sleeping space, but what we hadn't anticipated was the ambience. A pole connected to the wind generator ran straight from roof to sleeping mat. The ensuing agitation and wave slapping shook the entire bow of the boat and gave the exact impression of being in a washing machine. Or, to look at it more positively, a magic fingers bed on steroids. Fun!

In the men's cabin, the pole containing all of the essen-tials including the automatic pilot, ran through the cabin from the hatch to the frontmost point. Their accommodations were even more cramped than ours.

Due to the weight of the loaded boat, the cabins sat half below the waterline. When the frequent waves slammed us, water would cascade through the air vents, flooding every-thing. Permanently. This tiny five-person shared space was in a constant state of soddenness and condensation. During the night, more moisture slimed the walls, then rained back down on us. The water cycle—ugh. Our sleeping yoga mats were saturated, and sleeping in our foulies didn't really help.

The sea was loud. Every time a wave hit the boat, we'd get tossed off the sleeping bench. We learned to sleep curled up with an arm bracing our bodies to prevent us from sliding off the bench into the coffin. Day and night, we were jolted awake by incessant but irregular low-pitched growls from the automatic pilot. Felt like we were living inside a hungry stomach.

Seasickness, regardless of all the store-bought antidotes, bracelets, Dramamine, ear patches, canned peaches, was the absolute norm.

People dealt with their seasickness differently. Nabs couldn't function, so he tried to take refuge in the cabin. Not an option. Instead, forced back to his seat, he curled into himself and could not row. Jen, on the other hand, was stalwart, vomiting over the side between strokes.

We'd all find out later how these different ways of coping became almost archetypal. We all had our ways of facing life's challenges. Sometimes these differences were so pronounced it felt like we were living out some kind of crazy Broadway musical full of heroes and villains, caregivers and comic relief, misfits and frat boys and wannabe royalty.

February 1 (later)

Last night, a ghost ship, a freighter, appeared through the gloom — silent, eerie, a black behemoth shadow vague against the moonlit landscape of sea. It felt like an omen. Dolphins glided past at dawn.

Let's see···Colin's questions. What did I give to the boat? I was relatively cheerful.

What did I take? — I didn't want to talk. I was battling just to do my job as a rower.

W1 WEDNESDAY

The first hours of terror on the tumultuous sea, the darkness and seasickness, all abated enough by the second day that we started to use the sea for our own purposes: to go faster. This drive was both formidable and primitive. It felt like being in the Marines, where Sergeant Sea tore you down to see what you were made of. We wanted to be worthy of the sea's demands. We also wanted to crush it. The foolish and wishful confidence that we might get all the way through a shift relatively dry was smacked down with a wet slap every time we took our seats. It was always so dark given the clouds and rain and the curtains of waves encasing us.

The sea made its own landscape – towers and mountains. It gave us the finger or shook a fist at the Gods, the water plunging one minute, leaping skyward the next. In case you were wondering, the earth is undoubtedly round – a 360-degree horizon of clouds and sunrise and sunsets, a great blue dome above by day and universes of stars by night. Occasional ships passed by like spirits. One blew us a salute in bemusement or maybe admiration at the audacity of this very little cork bouncing in the sea.

The route across the North Atlantic is one of the busiest highways in the world. While the Vikings tackled the seas 500 years earlier, Columbus' passage from Europe to the Americas marked the beginning of all kinds of lucrative if ethically problematic trans-oceanic relationships. Upon the conquest of Manhattan, these soon-to-be-busy shipping lanes became instrumental in promoting trade between the New World and England along with the rest of Europe. For a long time, these shipping lanes represented the essential connections between continents. These days, though, freighter traffic has become much diminished.

It didn't take long to get over all those anxious pretenses around using the bucket as an open-air toilet. Those early hours of retching and followed by the necessity of baring one's bum to deal with rashes and sores superseded any kind of need for modesty. All rowers know intimately that rash you get on your bum and tailbone when intense rowing creates friction on the sliding seat. These painful indignations are exacerbated by moisture. What starts as an irritation can quickly develop into torture. Silver lining? We stopped worrying about exposing ourselves. The guys had no trouble at all, in fact, stripping down all the way. We, of course, were not allowed to follow (birthday) suit, but who needed a sunburn on top of all the other aches and pains?

By the end of our second day, it hurt so much to row that we were all leaning either on the rigging or our hands, rowing one-handed to take the pressure off our butts. The four-hour night watches were the hardest when, by the third hour, my hamstrings and butt were screaming at the merciless clock. There were times I felt I could not take another stroke. I could not sit there for one more second. But I did. This is what we were here for. Most of us were able to dig in deep and take that one more stroke, then another, and another. Most of us. Not all.

We were all attached to the boat with a surfer's leash, easily broken. At shift changes, we detached to crawl back to the cabins. Jen and Anna lived in their life jackets. I just tried to take it slow and steady.

Day 2

It is so terrifying at night because you can't see when a giant rogue wave is going to hit us broadside. When a wave comes over the whole boat and in the cabins, it sweeps you out of your seat and slams you furiously against the bow cabin or on the rigging. We are leashed in but so afraid we will go overboard.

You are swept right out of your shoes. 2 oars have broken and the foot stretchers. The seats are pulled right off the rails. The inserts of the crocs have become sodden lumps and have been thrown overboard.

It is much more dangerous than I imagined. Everything breaks before the onslaught of the sea. The ocean is so formidable and terrifying, a faceless giant shaking us in his fist like dice.

W1 THURSDAY

The morning dawned calmer, mercury seas, wind still a steady twenty knots. We were getting used to the rogue waves, 20-30 feet high, that swept over the side of the boat and soaked everything, again and again. Or maybe we were just getting used to the torment and panic. Thank God for foulies.

I thought a lot about the mantra I'd used so frequently with my kids, my constant playmates and excellent co-adventurers: "If you are scared of something, you have to do it once." So we made a habit of doing scary things. The second part of the mantra, "And then you have to do it again to prove that the first time was not a fluke," meant that we often did the scariest things again and again, just to prove...something...to ourselves. There were all kinds of spills and wrecks and Emergency Room visits and tears. But I never stopped believing in the basic premise.

But this. This race was certainly the most daunting and difficult and frightening enterprise I had ever undertaken. It was not fun. I guess if it were, well, where's the challenge in that?

People were starting to evolve into their innate selves. Nabs appeared to be so terrified and so weak that he hardly rowed. Once he was sent to our cabin, he miraculously healed. Yes, it was all completely overwhelming. Nabs just couldn't handle it. Jonathan, either. He was so special that he took a half hour off of our four-hour shift.

"Where are you going?" I asked, as he stowed his oar and crawled out of his seat.

"I'm fricking freezing," he mewled. "And my ass is hamburger."

"But..." I started.

Whatever, though. Did I really want to get into it with this guy? We all had sores on our asses. Indomitable Shaun was still vomiting, poor fellow. The whole boat smelled of brine and sour peaches.

We were on for the record, keeping pace with the Mondial, a boat that had left before us.

Day 3

Mood: slightly irritated but okay and acting cheerful.

Give to the boat: no complaints, rowing as best as I can in pain, not a grandstander

Take from the boat: a great admiration for the other equally nauseated and pained rowers.

I was primarily responsible for sending "news" to the Woodvale website. Apparently, this tidbit got a strong response:

While acting as bow ballast, 6'7" 300 lb. Roger daintily slipped overboard to panicked cries of "MAN OVERBOARD." Always levelheaded, Shaun came to the rescue. Efforts to grab Roger by the hair were thwarted as he is

bald, but Shaun coolly pulled Roger abroad by his life jacket strap. But for a few nicks and bruises and a much-needed sea bath, Roger was fine.

As he recovered from his plunge it was clear to see that Roger was nursing his leg and knee, his head bowed with pain and regret. He'd hyper-extended his knee in the plunge and was distressed and embarrassed he couldn't row. He confided in me that he couldn't stand the idea that we "had to lug his 300 pounds around," and he seemed ashamed. Totally decimated emotionally, in fact. As his knee swelled, he dragged himself off the deck and into the women's cabin where he squeezed into the coffin to be out of the way. Nobody resented him at all, and our sympathy was profound.

On the flip side, the sun came out for the first time that morning. It was wonderful. And the evening shift was fun. Finally, no one was sick, so everyone razzed to surf waves. We heard we were neck and neck with La Mondial.

I had been refusing my snack pack as I had never been big on candy. I gave most of it to skinny Shaun, who needed the food. In exchange, he'd eat all the candy and nuts out of his snack pack and leave me the raisins. But, as the end of Week One approached, I decided to keep my chocolate bars, mostly out of boredom. The energy boost helped, too.

Day 3 (later)

The days are starting to melt together. The cabin is a disaster with up to five people in a space hardly big enough for two or three. Everything is soaked, and it's always fun trying to sleep in what feels like a green-house in the heart of the jungle.

Mood: Whatever

Gave: Rowed my ass off

Took: My own chocolate bars back. For the first time in my life, I'm not worried about getting fat. This is a new way of thinking for me, banishing the lifelong eating disordered thinking. It is a new way of thinking, "you are what you are." I can't decide if I feel liberated or just···too tired to do it anymore.

W1 FRIDAY

The four-hour night shifts were the hardest. It was just so dark, you couldn't see anything, a very strange feeling. Plus, I was annoyed with Nabs and Jonathan for their unwillingness to actually row. Simon was furious. Jonathon was never ready to come on shift, and his prima donna attitude regarding the gift of his presence on board was starting to wear on everyone. Still, it felt like we were clipping along beautifully.

That morning, Ben and I wanted to surf the waves. This was the best feeling in the world. With the coordinated effort of the crew, we could reach the crest and catch an electrifying ride to the bottom of the swell. The trick is that everyone needed to pull hard to get up there to the top of the wave. For some reason, Jonathan and Dan just would not turn up the power. Beth, too, had succumbed to the vapors, apparently, and couldn't function. I was too exhausted to push the issue and instead became internally disgruntled with her. I was near tears and so wet and grumpy from lack of sleep. There were cuts and bruises all over our bodies, all of which had become minorly infected. And my ass hurt like I had been sitting on a frying pan.

Still, with the two of us in the stroke seats, Ben and I could surf up to six knots. It was exhilarating. The perfect antidote to internal disgruntlement and lame teammates.

Day 4

I had a dream the rudder was broken and we were aborting and being towed to Africa. I awoke, woke the others, and convinced everyone it was true. We were all so glad and grateful that we had an unimpeachable way out until Ben noted Simon had not told us that as he had not been in the cabin. I was so disappointed. Wishful thinking.

Mood; grumpy, exasperated, irritable.

Gave: hard rowing

Took: impatience

Where does the saying "pulling your own weight" come from? Interestingly it is a rowing/crew instruction where each member of a crew must pull on an oar at least hard enough to propel his or her own bodyweight. Hmm.

W1 SATURDAY

My team, Team A as ordained by Simon, were a bunch of misfits. His group, Team B, were the normals. I had 'team envy."

Mine was a group of misfits, a few of whom seemed to always be looking for ways to shirk. Why were they even here? Okay, okay. Only a couple of us really knew what we were getting into. I could try to be a little kinder. But shit. I was definitely losing patience.

Beth insisted on stroking, but refused to pull hard or surf the waves. She insisted that she'd signed on to row, not river raft. But why not, when the reward for working hard to climb the wave sent us screaming down the other side of it?

If this woman mentions her vagina one more time, I thought, I will scream. Beth had zero boundaries and was a practicing hypochondriac. We knew all about every infection in all parts of her body.

"I have to groom myself, right now," she'd announce in the cabin. "Even – no, especially – my vagina." She giggled at Shaun. "I hope it's okay," she purred, splaying her legs and examining every nook and cranny.

I wondered if she'd been raised in a convent or something, repressed as a child, finally liberated. I swear poor Shaun sat there with his eyes covered.

Nabs, our resident Saudi prince, looked as if he hated being there. While he certainly described himself as an adventurer and had, indeed, accomplished all kinds of risky feats, he acted as though being treated as a galley slave (face the facts, man) were beneath his position. Maybe it was the seasickness that was really destroying him. That beast was cruel.

My team was clearly the "Breakfast Club" next to Team B's "Popular Kids."

In the '80s movie, *The Breakfast Club*, a group of students has to spend a Saturday in detention. It's a ragbag of dysfunctional archetypes. There's the thug, the socialite, the nerd, the weirdo. At first, they're all either intimidated or suspicious or superior or too cool for each other. In the movie, they eventually work it out.

The cool kids sang and worked together, and all had pirate pet names for each other. Our team was disjointed riff raff. I could feel the envy steaming out of all of our pores.

Roger–Team B, of course–was such a good guy. Because of his knee, he couldn't row. Instead of complaining about it, he made us breakfast. We loved him for it.

We finally figured out how to get the sitting water mostly out of the cabin (so it didn't condense and rain back on us), and to straighten the place up a bit. Everyone would just lie on the benches in there with their butts exposed, rashes and sores and infected boils and cuts airing out. What we needed was sunshine.

Day 5

First sleep in several days.

Gave: hard rowing

Took: impatience

Mood: Only three more weeks.

W1 SUNDAY

I thought we'd fixed the leaks in the hull, but more water must have gotten in through the pumps belowdecks. A lot of the food got soaked, so we cleaned what we could and tossed the rest overboard. I had to force myself to retain confidence in Simon, even if it meant fastidiously ignoring the obvious.

After much scuttlebutt–loud complaints, actually–about Team A (us), Roger came to observe. He inserted himself right in and fit perfectly, which is apparently one of his many gifts. Of course, everyone was pulling together to kick ass, so it was not the worst example of our dysfunction. Sometimes it just takes one dynamic individual to pull a whole group together, and that day, Roger was it. Still, he saw right through our best behavior. I could tell he was pretty disgusted with us. Sad.

Day 6

I am not getting any messages. I know there are messages. We were promised as our friends and family
wrote in to the web site Kate would read us messages
daily via the SAT phone. Nothing. I cannot believe no
one has written···

W1 MONDAY

One week. One week that felt like three months. I was so physically weary and tired of coping that it was nearly impossible to
get up. I lay in bed numb and thoughtless.

But Shaun was cooking and my butt felt a little better, so
I stretched my body as long as I could on the bench, then
crawled on deck for shift change. We were no longer on a
rotating schedule. We'd shifted, instead, just to Team A and
Team B, six people rowing and one cook per shift. I requested
not to cook if others would rather as I did not want a day's rest.
I was here to row.

The new method was safer and more regular, but it meant
that we rarely had contact with the other team, and the boat
became even more divided.

I told myself to stop being so judgmental. Everyone was
tired, I knew, and probably a little scared. Jonathan took more
than 1.5 hours in breaks in a 2.5-hour watch. Beth spoke only
of her vagina and her nakedness. I didn't say much, but I knew
my face gave me away—disdain, anger, heart of stone. Maybe
I should have thought of them as my kids. But my kids, truly,
were light years cooler. Be less petty, I reminded myself again.
And again.

Day 7

Disappointed we are 86 hours behind Team Hallin. We question where to go, how to find the Trades.

I washed and bandaged Roger's leg and foot. His knee is woefully swollen and hot to the touch. Very fearful of an infection.

Mood? Happy because we are in a big east-west wind.

Gave: Let's see. At 1000 strokes per hour, twelve hours per day···my soul?

Took: Nothing. Really. It's kind of a one-way street (shipping lane?) these days.

8

Week Two

"We're all pretty bizarre. Some of us are just better at hiding it, that's all."

The Breakfast Club

W2 TUESDAY

The watch system was not complicated. The teams alternated, one on, one off, 24 hours a day. This was the original scheme, cleverly concocted by, who else, Anna. For example:

First shifts:
    Team A, 6:00 a.m. – 9:00 a.m.
    Team B, 9:00 a.m. – 12:00 a.m.

Second and third shifts:
    Team A, 12:00 a.m. – 2:30
    Team B, 2:30 p.m. – 5:00 p.m.
    Team A, 5:00 p.m. – 7:30 p.m.
    Team B, 7:30 p.m. – 10:00 p.m.

And the dreaded night shifts:
    Team A, 10:00 p.m. – 2:00 a.m.
    Team B, 2:00 a.m. – 6:00 a.m.

Night shift was a death march. Four-hour rests were required to preserve REM sleep, but sleep was nearly impossible. The hallucinations continued: driving down country lanes, seeing ghosts, the unshakable conviction that we were rowing in circles, etc.

Nabs, it was reported, nodded off while rowing and fell out of his seat.

> **Mike** is a Brit, a fireman doing this row for charity. Mike rowed like a madman, totally hard core. Grey haired, lean muscular body, he is a gnarly guy with a terrible northern accent. He speaks only in pronouncements, like "fuck you." Gruffy, kind, and thoughtful, the guy is an inspiration: not a grandstander, but sedulous in his efforts. He is quite unhappy about being here in this physically compromised state (his oar grip was so tight, he had probably damaged his ulnar nerve, which would explain the cramped fingers and claw hand. And his butt rash–the absolute worst), but his frankly described assessments were just honest, never devious or whiny.

I got lucky this morning and actually slept for an hour. When I woke up and got back to the oar, I felt refreshed and chatty.

"You know what I've been wondering," I announced to anyone who wasn't plugged in. "Where are the whales? Shouldn't they be all over the place?" Yes, I was a mountain girl at that point, but I'd spent enough time near the ocean to know that it was migration season somewhere in the Atlantic. No humpbacks?

Mike's response hit hard. "They are south, in the trades. They know it's scrambled eggs up here. That's why no one else is here."

Trade Winds: What are the trade winds, and why did we have to find them? The winds, the Easterlies, blow from east to west and they have an impact on the current. In fact, Columbus owes his trans-Atlantic successes to the "Votta de Mare," as do other European (and later, American) colonizers and traders. In case you're interested, Columbus' first journey to the "West Indies" took about three months, from the Canary Islands to what he believed was Asia (but was actually the Caribbean). The trades flow in the Equatorial region and strengthen during the winter, which explains why these races happen January-March. Well, that and no hurricanes.

No one else was here? He was right. In the middle of the Atlantic there is very little sea life – we saw no whales or dolphins, there were no sea birds. We had not found the trade winds nor the Columbus West-East current that would have assisted us in making an easier run across the ocean. We kept searching, aiming a little more north one day, a little more south the next, a much more circuitous route than going straight forward. We even asked cargo ship navigators and yacht captains where they might have found it. Nothing worked, we just couldn't find the currents. We were rowing exclusively under human power.

That evening, 31 days after they'd left the Canaries, Team Hallin broke the world record for the fastest Atlantic crossing. Big Blue broke theirs ten hours later. Great news for them, but we were dispirited knowing we would not be record breakers. Shoot. Still, we had to keep rowing hard. There were plenty of reasons for this, but one stood out: we had no choice.

Day 8

It is not unusual for me to be in a situation where motivations are different. But some of these people are just extraordinarily different from me. I guess I'm just wondering how I ended up here. I really have to figure out how to cope, with less anger and resentment.

But right now, I'm in a foul humor; fighting with Beth regarding space. She has to extend her legs and groom and we, crumpled as we are, are in her way. I am very sick of the entitlement, but it will all work out.

The weather is flat and windless. We are rowing hard. It was a good session last night with Ben and Shaun. Smooth as can be. We are heading for the trades!

I am so homesick.

Music on deck and rowing heralded warm sunny days and warmer dry nights. The crew's mood elevated as each shed their damp foulies and literally bared wounds to the healing sun.

W2 THURSDAY

The day dawned relatively calm, but currents felt weird, like they were fighting us, and the rowing was a lot of work for little gain.

Dan, apparently, had decided against pushing himself too hard. Instead, he tucked the oar handle under his knee, stretched his arms lazily over his head, then leaned on the gunwale looking south like a pretty mistress enjoying a leisurely rowboat tour of the Plaza de Espana.

The conversation was even more absurd and offensive than usual. It didn't take long before all three of the guys were taking a break, cracking each other up. Sex, kink, women's (and men's) waxing preferences, body shapes—suddenly, nothing was off limits. And why not, I asked myself? Why shouldn't they be able to talk about whatever they wanted?

Because...they weren't rowing. And I was tired. And disgusted.

"Hey, Dan," I couldn't help it. "How about you shut up and row a little instead of showing the world what an asshole you are?" That's it. I said it. Catch. Drive. Finish. Return.

Dan turned and stared at me, mouth agape. In all our weeks together, no one had ever seen me mad.

The guys were obviously irked. He grabbed his oar with a grumble and slapped it in the water without considering the timing. When his oar bashed mine, he acted like it was my fault.

I focused on my breathing, the rhythmic thunk of oar in oarlock, the army of red blood cells churning through my circulatory system.

We needed some help from Simon. Later that day, I pulled him aside and, without telling tales or complaining, I just explained that we needed some encouragement and some guidance. His cream-of-the-crop team had little direct contact with our Breakfast Club, but if he could just talk to us, give our team some of the same encouragement he gave his own? We needed his leadership. Without it, I feared, Team A would never figure out how to work together or feel part of the boat.

Day 10

I sent a hopeful "news flash" to the website via Simon:

Britannia Teams A & B locked in Battle

Long known for its solidarity, jocularity and high jinks in wave surfing, Team B was finally challenged by a recently re-organized Team A. Shifts are now defined by fierce competition. Team B leads by a slight edge; Team A predicts giving Team B a good thrashing. We'll see if writing it down makes it real.

I called home yesterday. It was so delightful to have a brief hello and what's up. SAT phones are too expensive for more than that.

W2 FRIDAY

It felt as if we'd been at sea for months. Each day stretched longer than the one before in a hamster wheel of row, sleep, eat. One day slid into another, defined not by the rising and setting sun, but only by shifts, two hours on, two hours off, three on, three off, and on and on. Each crew member rowed twelve hours a day.

Day 11's night was a "runner." We did seven knots in the 10-2 a.m. shift. It was like whitewater rafting, where you rappel off the water, catching waves and making each oar stroke count. After that, during the 2-6 a.m. shift, the wind picked up. The waves grew deadly, the ocean rising like a stampede of wild horses, sharp hooves grabbing, mouths foaming, running faster and higher. During the last hour of their shift, I heard the other team trying to distract themselves with games like "I see a color…" There just weren't many colors to choose from.

Roger was struggling. His knee put him totally out of commission. Simon put him out of harm's way (and ours) by sending him down to our cabin's "coffin," an awful place where he had to tuck in under the deck so that only his head and chest were free. I couldn't even think about the human detritus down there, bandages and salt and…skin.

Day 12

I swear to God, Anna and Jen are obsessed with where I stow my yellow bag, but what am I supposed to do? Stowing is a pain in the ass as you have to pull up the yoga mats and open the hatches. I use my little bag as a pillow, and it is hardly a big deal, but it pisses them off. And I am feeling petty. They are even more dismayed that Roger is there during their sleep shift, and poor Roger, he cannot with any facility climb in and out. He is laid out in the coffin day and night. I would go crazy.

Instead, I get to feel lucky. Today there are big swells and I am pretty cheerful. I want to send messages to everyone at home.

Most of the crew has boils. Lucky me, I don't (yet).

Glory! Tonight's sunset was dazzling, water reflecting ochre with black tips, like a lion's pelt. There should be as many different names for waves as Eskimos have

for snow, as the color, texture, consistency and movement changes not only day to day, but shift to shift.
We skimmed along.

W2 SUNDAY

The crying days were the worst. Conditions were harrowing,
giant waves crashing over the decks, swallowing everything
and knocking us out of our seats. We were all freezing cold
and soaked to the bone. We had to pull out the damp foulies
to cope.

It was one of those days when simply controlling the oar
was a nasty challenge. Jonathon was sitting next to me, on
port. Suddenly, a wave lifted up my oar and shoved it into
Jon-athon's space. He grabbed the handle and shoved it back—
right into my shins.

"Ouch!" I yelped. "SHIT!"

Jonathon said nothing, just sat there yanking his oar and
glowering.

A few minutes later, it happened again.

"Sorry! Sorry!" I gasped, trying to get the oar back under
control.

This time, Jonathon turned his face to me and watched
as he slammed the oar into my shins again. "Don't you ever,
EVER, let that happen again!" he screamed.

I could hardly breathe from the pain. Had anyone noticed
this cruelty? I looked around. No one seemed to care at all.
Maybe they were all just drowning in their own misery.

Now, I was a woman who worked for women's rights.
I'd raised two excellent children, steering them through thick
and thin like a champ. I'd survived a challenging childhood
and professionally witnessed abuse in some of its worst
forms. Was I willing just to let this go?

"Why did you do that?" I asked.

He didn't even turn his head, just kept rowing. So did I. So tired.

Day 13

No messages yet, though I know my dear friends and family are sending notes to the website. Called home — My daughter scored in her interview at Brown. She is trying to get into a PhD program in Neurosciences and it looks as if she will make it somewhere. I am so proud of her.

W2 MONDAY

Evening, 4-hour watch. We were *flying*, perfect rowing on a liquid mountain landscape. Felt like running with bulls or, even better, with wolves: fast and furious as the waves thundered along with the boat in their grasp. At the end of each watch, we challenged ourselves to row a 5K as if we were actually in a race. Such an uplifting way to wrap up the effort. It was beautiful and cool and exciting, and I retired to my cabin feeling powerful and triumphant.

Roger was there, his infected knee elevated but so swollen. I'd talked to Simon earlier in the day, worried that the medication we had to offer was insufficient, that Roger should be in the hospital. Simon vowed to call the doctor.

I was blue-lipped and shivering during my "sleep" break. Dear Roger hunched next to me, round face and shiny bald pate mirroring the moon behind him.

"You look cold," his warm-hearted voice resonated. "Here, wear this." He slipped the luxurious velour pullover, XXL, over my head.

Purring with gratitude, I snuggled into the cocoon. Roger stayed close, a dear caretaker, then began singing a medley of

American and British pop, his rich baritone crooning us all to sleep. I was overcome by his kindness.

Day 14

It's Valentine's Day, but love is definitely not in the air.

Beth has been obsessing about her boils and how she cannot stretch her legs and that she wants to be in the aft cabin (with a new audience and with the men). She's set up boundaries for us so that there is no encroachment in her space and although we ALL are curled up LIKE FETUSES, now no one can stretch their legs. we all are in pain. Beth, evidently, feels she is a special case.

Simon finally gave in to Beth's peppering him with complaints and requests. Exasperated, he sent her to the forward cabin. YESSSS. Total luxury for Shaun and me and poor Roger in the coffin.

Called family for Valentine's day. I want them all to know how much I love them.

9

Week Three

Simple Pleasures and Stolen Socks

Morning had finally arrived. We'd rowed for hours in a good glide. During the last hour we played games and laughed. Laughing made a huge difference. Changed everything. But then Jonathan popped back into nasty form, mean, and we fell back into the Team A blues. What a drag.

Roger was the opposite of Jonathon. He was diagnosed by a physician via SAT phone with "housemaid's knee," so phew, I could stop worrying. We laughed that in his other life, he was called Shrek. He continued to sing us to sleep, and it was so lovely.

I was getting a lot better at something I'd been trying to do all my life. I'd learned to think of nothing. I rowed when I was on watch, looked at photos from the girls during the off-hours. Appreciated the sun, when it was out. Watched the waves.

Every once in a while, I'd amuse myself by metaphorically rocking the boat.

Dan was consistent in one way: he rowed erratically, in tune not to the rhythm of the strokes, but to the music in his earbuds. He didn't even seem to try to keep any kind of cadence. Staying in sync with the stroke really is the #1 rule of rowing. If rowers move together, the boat moves. If we don't, the boat jerks around like a jalopy on a dirt road. Everyone works harder just to make headway. Dan must have known this.

"Hey, Dan," I chirped one chilly morning. "How's it going?"

I didn't want to start a fight. Instead of begging him—again—to be part of the team, I went in a side door: "Is the trim okay?" Trim refers to the balance of the boat, everyone rowing together with equivalent power.

"Yeah," he replied, not getting it. He wasn't even rowing. He didn't know and didn't care. But I enjoyed a wee laugh at his expense, which kept me going for another hour.

Even after I discovered that my iPod was ruined since someone left it unplugged and in a puddle, I thought of nothing. The sun was out.

Even while Team B took all kinds of photos and movies so that the battery was always dead for our watch, I thought of nothing. The sun was out.

Was I always a picture of equanimity? Hell no.

One cold and rainy day, I couldn't understand why my foulie was so uncomfortable. I was having trouble rowing in it, and it kept catching in the wheels of the sliding seat. I was a size Small, and this tent was decidedly Large. Had I taken someone else's? I checked the name tag. No name. I know I'd written my name on the collar of my foulie.

"Anyone seen my coat," I asked the crew. "I'm wearing the wrong one here. It doesn't fit."

DAMN.

"Can I just check yours, just to make sure?" A few grunts of assent were all I needed. I didn't bother with the guys since my Small wouldn't have fit them anyway. Anna's didn't have a name in it. "Thanks," I smiled. "Sorry to bug."

Beth's wasn't mine.

Jen seemed a little squirmy. Yup. There was my name on the collar of the coat she was wearing.

"Hey!" Did I sound friendly enough? "This is my foulie. How funny,...right?"

"Oh yeah, oops," she giggled. "I took your jacket the first day. Mine didn't fit right, so I borrowed yours." She shrugged.

"You borrowed it?" I was no longer thinking of nothing. "You should have asked." I took off the foulie I was wearing and waited for her to do the same. She did so. To call her capitulation grudging would be an understatement.

"Have you taken anything else of mine?"

She looked at her feet.

"Hey! Those are my wool socks!" I'd been looking everywhere for them. I only had two pairs, one for rowing, and one for changing into after a wet row. My feet had been cold and soaked for days. She'd had them for three days. I was dumbfounded.

The truth is, I would have lent anyone anything if they'd asked, and did so frequently. My job in life, it seemed, was to keep the peace and try to make everyone happy. But this assault on my comfort felt so unfair. So why was she the one acting so pissed off?

At least it felt good to have a foulie that fit and a pair of dry socks. At least that. And the sun would come out again eventually, I was sure.

Day 15

Simon seemed annoyed when I asked for the messages we were promised since I have not received any and only have contact if I can reach someone by SAT phone. I learned that we are not to get any of the Woodvale messages as it is too expensive and the only way we can hear from anyone is if they call or text by SAT phone. That felt duplicitous and like a bait and switch. I cannot communicate with my supportive friends, cannot hear their messages, but at least I feel mollified by the fact that there are messages there.

Simon is part Peter Pan and part Lord of the Flies. I am annoyed watching Jen suck up to him, so much head shaking and flirting. Their group, the Spartans (Team B), talk like normal people and share and converse. They have lecture series and play games. They are almost all Brits. We are more disparate. Roger blames himself and his depression for not unifying the crew and also blames Jonathan's divisiveness. I ask myself what role I've played in the poisonous group dynamic.

Do I like who I am being? My innate joyfulness has diminished. I am working on no anger, but inside, it's not working. I actually can sit and seethe and monitor people in what they are doing or not doing. I think it is partly about the whole Catholic "not good enough" message meted out as currency by my parents (and everyone else). I also think a lot about Mike and loss. It consumes me at times. And it must stop.

W3 WEDNESDAY

We ended our shift in first place: 1000 miles down! Yay! We were awesome. It wasn't easy. We rowed race style to make that 1000-mile mark. Push, pull, glide, return. Push, pull, glide, return...a terrific effort put in by all. A milestone in the dark. We were elated.

W3 THURSDAY

The day started with Team A at the helm. Most of us preferred this 2-6 a.m. shift—it was always easier to witness the arrival of the dawn rather than to push on into the darkest of the wee hours. We passed the time telling stories. They begged me to regale them with the saga of a criminal defendant who was not guilty but received a life sentence anyway. We, his legal team, were eventually able to set him free.

The legal system in the United States is messy and flawed and amazing. As a psychologist specializing in forensics, I had the good fortune to be involved with astonishingly competent and passionate public defenders and private defense attorneys involved with an Innocence Project type of case. These are teams of lawyers and other advocates whose work to prevent and correct wrongful convictions has righted hundreds of judicial wrongs since their inception in the 1990's. I had already practiced as an expert witness in death penalty cases, and as a mitigation expert, and now was asked to be part of this team. We were finally able to prove that this man was indeed wrongfully convicted and was subsequently freed due to the diligent work of his team.

The crew could hardly believe their ears. To think anyone could be hauled out of bed and thrown in jail on a whim or a data error—no one wanted to believe it. Shaun said the story gave him nightmares.

I was smacked in the head by a flying fish, which sounds funny, I know, but it also hurt. A lot. As a consolation prize, though, I got to wash my hair! With water! For real! We had all been allotted one bottle of water to do so, and I was ecstatic to finally use mine. Wow, did it feel good.

In some ways, we were all starting to tune in more closely to the simple pleasures.

We each needed 8,000 calories to row twelve hours a day. Mueslix for breakfast was the closest we got to fresh food. The raspberry crumble was so delicious, sweet and tart, real fruit combined with a delightful crunch. It was everyone's favorite. Lamb pilaf for lunch. Chili con carne for dinner. Peronin, a heavily supplemented "liquid food," turned into late-night pudding.

The chili was tough. The hot water never quite softened the beans, so it was always a little crunchy, which resulted in some gastro-intestinal distress and, ahem, boat-wide flatulence. Embarrassing, but what could we do? Just laugh, like a bunch of fourth-grade boys.

We celebrated Shaun's birthday by giving him the 8-10 a.m. shift off.

"No way," he said, his voice a bit shaky. "You can manage without me for two hours?" It meant he could sleep until noon. I thought he might start crying.

We laughed. "Happy birthday, Shaun." He was adorable.

Six hours later, he crawled out of the cabin and gasped. Team B had smuggled a flattish, rumpled chocolate store-bought cake, quite the worse for wear all the way from Porto Mogan, and it was laid out on deck surrounded by a few soggy presents: two toy swords, a pirate bandanna, and a stuffed parrot, all in celebration of the team's pirate proclivities. We each had a sporkful of cake and played 21 Questions, discussed the British monarchy, IKEA, and Lego. Man, it was good to laugh. These were smart, funny people. When things went well, life was good.

Day 17

Mike wrote yesterday and apparently lost my cats, Nimbles and White. I am so sad and angry but trying not to lay blame. Called and left a message to find the kitties. It makes me so sad and worried.

Jen was exhausted so she had to miss her shift and slept in our cabin last night, which meant mediocre sleep for everyone due to overcrowding.

I have small infections on every digit. Ugly. Guess I will never get to do a commercial for beautiful hands.

Where are the trades?

Why don't feet dry?

W3 FRIDAY

The sun was out and it was warm, finally. The sea was calm, and we took a break from rowing for a mid-Atlantic swim. I didn't go in because it was too cold and I am such a weenie, but everyone else went in—naked, of course. So many penises I had to laugh.

I had to text Mike: "so many penises and—," but the end of the sentence got cut off. Mike, the joker, evidently sent out an email to my friends to "finish the sentence." My college room-mate, Pam, hit it right on the nose: "so many penises but what good are they....at least they are inflatable."

We also cleaned the boat beneath the waterline by scraping off the barnacles and seaweed with plastic cups.

The rest of the day was slow going, eight hard miles in the three-hour afternoon session. Saw a buoy adrift. Cereal, chili con carne. Finally, our team was able to rectify the SAT phone issues and we were receiving select messages from afar, and it was lovely to hear from Mike and my sister Debbie – they were all making bets on our date of arrival. We were that close?

The evening watch saw pilot whales, a pod of three. The Popular Kid team hollered and we all clambered on deck to see them cavorting about 25 feet off deck, their sleek, burnished arcs emerging and then melting into the waves. Then, a moonrise, rosy, as large as a sun swallowing the horizon.

Day 18

Excellent news!!! My daughter got into grad school — we talked today and I am so proud. BC and Brown and waiting for Harvard. They said she was the best candidate they ever had. Waiting to hear.

And hooray! We FINALLY packed the foulies away into the storage under the benches (we call it the Hendersons)!!! It seems the storms and the cold are over, and we are heading toward warmer weather where we can be comfortable with regular jackets. Finally, we can perhaps not have the cabins so filled with water and wet and stink.

Over time we have become acclimated to the terrible odors of unwashed bodies and hair, flatulence, the bucket, and brine on people and in the cabins. I've even gotten used to Jen's rebuffs and nastiness. Is it a good thing, to stop caring? It is dawning on me that I am pretty hypersensitive and perhaps read too much into the behavior of others. Great for a psychologist, not so great as a person. Either way, it's a relief to stop sweating the details.

W3 SATURDAY

Grey overcast morning. Medium sea. The sun broke on the horizon, a shimmering oasis just out of reach extending a golden carpet to seduce us to magic Summerland. Then back to grey. My butt was bleeding, so I changed into a sarong–less friction.

I decided to try harder to resist the internal Jonathan bashing. Just because he was a weenie didn't make it okay or even satisfying for me to try to get him to pull his weight. He could pull it or not, his choice. I wasn't going to change him, to turn him into a decent fellow who wanted to help out the team even if it meant sacrificing his own comfort. Being annoyed with him only added to the suffering. No point in that.

Beth hadn't yet figured out the secret about not whining.

"I hate this so much," she pouted, pulling her oar like a three-year-old. "And it's never going to end, is it? We'll be on this fucking ocean together, staring at each other's bloody butts, for the rest of our lives, won't we?" Who was she talking to? Everyone? No one? Just me?

"Let me ask you this," I started. "It's something I've been asking myself a lot. Why do you think you were put on this boat?"

She tilted her head and shrugged.

"And part two," I continued. "What are you supposed to learn from the experience?"

She nodded. "Yeah, good questions." Shifting in her seat, she adjusted her grip and leaned back, using her legs to push. It had been a while since I'd seen such a solid stroke out of her. She grimaced–I could tell the boils were so painful, and I felt for her–but kept on, catching and driving like she meant it. She didn't have to answer my question out loud. She was thinking about it, I could tell. So was I.

I still didn't have any boils – yet – probably due to the

bacterial immunity I must have developed over the years living with four dogs, two cats, a couple of adventurous children, and clients from all walks of life. Guy had them all over his body, huge suppurating sores that broke and bled all over the seats. The others, too, especially the ones who seemed to come from the cleanest kinds of lives, curated and healthy and sterile, seemed to be suffering the worst. I guess there might be something to be said for a little mud in the water, if you know what I mean.

Day 19

Totally dark night end of watch, beginning of another. No moon and cloud cover. Dark can be disorienting. Little sleep due to a low-pitched irregular but loud noise like thunder or a hungry stomach. We lurch.

Woke to harrowing 20-knot winds and horrific, painfully large waves breaking over the port side. Our night shift was terrifying and tearful and excruciating. We had to resurrect the foulies from the hold. And, when I finally staggered back into the cabin, no sleep was available until morning. We were simply too crowded. Beth had had a spat with Dan, so there were four of us squeezed onto benches, getting tossed against the cabin walls and into each other. Too much. Jonathan had a temper tantrum and abused some equipment.

The sun snuck up the next morning, like it always did. No one had really slept, and the vibe was like an electric cable buzzing in the rain, ready to pop.

Beth sniffled and covered her eyes with her hand. "I just don't understand why he has to be so mean," she croaked. "I do anything he wants, and still he doesn't take me seriously." She wiped her nose on her shirt.

This "therapy talk" would be a good way to get my mind

off how pissed I was at everyone, so I engaged. "Have you ever considered that he might respect you more if you didn't let him have his way all the time?" This felt so obvious, I was almost embarrassed to say it.

"What do you mean?" she asked, staring at me wide-eyed while I rowed and she didn't. "Why would he like me more if I said no to him?"

It seemed clear to me that Dan neither liked nor respected her. The woman had absolutely no boundaries when it came to sex talk, and she painted a picture of herself as a wild and crazy sexpot with enormous appetites and skills. In fact, this was one of her favorite topics of conversation. The fact that Dan egged her on while she was talking trash, then bullied and harassed her off shift – and she took it – made clear to anyone who was watching that both these people had a lot to learn about themselves.

"If you think about it," and here I was trying to be gentle, I really was, "is it possible for you to imagine what you yourself really want? I mean, for yourself? Not for him or any other guy?"

At last, she started rowing again. "Yeah, yeah, I know. I should be a liberated woman like you, not caring what the men think."

Was she being mean? I'd spent my life trying not to worry about what other people thought, but mostly failing in the attempts. I, like most of the women I knew, put way too much stock in whether or not we were attractive enough, thin enough, sparkly enough to capture some guy's attention. I guess maybe it was just luck that I'd been raised to have enough self-respect not to let that need for assurance get in the way of my physical and emotional safety.

"I care what people think," I replied.

She scoffed. "You're saying I'm stupid, right? To take it? I bet you took plenty of it, too, when you were my age." She was looking at me as if she really wanted to know.

"I had to learn," I admitted. "To say no to their bullshit."

She nodded. Wiped her eye with the back of her gloved hand. "I'm not sure I can do that."

Garbage – the sea is full of it. It was distressing to see the flotsam of human existence floating by, even out here in the middle of the ocean. This had been an issue from the beginning of the trip, the fact we had to add to the destruction of the ocean by dumping our trash. Simon had a point: we couldn't carry garbage in this boat. The bacteria from spoiled food alone could be dangerous. But the ocean was already rife with islands of trash. We lamented seeing garbage from what must have been other ocean rows. We feared being ramrodded by containers fallen off of ships or by other large refuse.

It's a terrible shame, what humans have done to this oceanic wilderness. Most people have heard of the garbage patch known as the North Atlantic Gyre. One study estimated that eight million metric tons of trash per year get dumped into the world's oceans. Of course, it kills animals and damages reefs, and it just keeps growing and growing. Yes, scientists are hard at work on solutions—thank you, NOAA! But dammit. There is no escape.

W3 SUNDAY

10-12 a.m. watch. Squall to south pushed us north. Good stroke port. Mueslix, coffee, shepherd's pie for lunch.

Twenty days in. I used to wish I was a whitewater raft guide, and here I was. This was larger and better than being a whitewater rafter, and I got to do it twelve hours a day. It was wild and crazy, riding the waves and battling the ocean cascading over you.

I used to wish for a lot of things. But it was on Day 20 that I realized I wanted no more "if onlies" in my life. Maybe this is what I was supposed to be learning: You are who you are.

Day 20

Night fell like an ambush. The darkest nights are the scariest. The moon was slow to rise behind a cloud. It's 2:00 a.m. Slow sea and grey. Checked for bats.

There are two little phrases that keep popping up in my head: "to suffer fools lightly" and "ship of fools." Need to know where they come from. Will text mike. I asked everyone on board and no one knows.

We were all so tired, no energy, but the flares for Mike Palmer's birthday were very cool. Strawberry chocolate crumble for late shift. Omigod, our favorite.

W3 MONDAY

The next morning dawned a steely grey, but heated up soon enough. I was happy to move from port side to starboard. Everyone was grateful to rotate seats. Rowing too long on one side led to severe tendonitis. We were all feeling it hard. Still, the rowing was slow, only 2-3 knots.

I could tell that Simon was disappointed in us. There is really not much in the world I like less than that feeling of letting someone down. That evening in the cabin, I had to ask.

"Hey, Simon." I felt like a kid working up the courage to talk to the teacher about missing homework.

He looked up at me, curious.

"I'm sorry about our pace, the record." I don't think he

and I had ever made such intense eye contact. "How can we do better?"

He nodded and shook his head, then smiled. "Pinto, you have nothing to be sorry about. You're working your ass off out there." He patted my arm, leaned in.

Yep, that's all I needed. My apprehension evaporated in his grin.

"Well," he continued, "the weather has not been friendly, that's a big part of it. And," he narrowed his eyes, "a few of your teammates just aren't pulling very hard. As you well know." Then he shrugged. This man, who'd crossed the ocean six times already, who'd put his heart and soul and marriage and family and life savings on the line for this opportunity, was able to shrug it off. I didn't always love Simon, but this overt embrace of a Very Large World View was impressive, just what I needed at that moment.

Back on deck, Roger started to sing, then we all joined in. Porridge, beef Bolognese and chili.

10

Week Four

Halfway Home

Week 4 was when I learned how to sleep. Dreamt of being a galley slave on a river. Then, that Beth had hidden her food in the toilet and it overflowed and I had to clean it all up. I woke up with a jolt and threw my clothes on, anxious not to miss a shift, or even be late. Why was everyone else still sleeping? They'd have been grateful to me for waking them up in a panic, except that we'd all only been asleep for two hours. I had dreamt the call. Embarrassing. Also, not uncommon. I crawled back into bed, but sleep refused to crawl in there with me.

Consolation prize: astonishing creamsicle sunrise. The sun was so large, oozing out of a mountain range of water. Foulies be gone.

Mueslix for breakfast. My ass hurt.

I spent the shift thinking about anger. I realized I found anger terrifying. I spent a lot of time and energy trying to be so perfect that no one had any reason to be angry with me. Not just now, in the middle of the Atlantic, but everywhere and always. Anger meant, at best, tight-lipped disapproval and, at worst, emotional abandonment. I could never allow anyone to be angry with me.

But on this cruise, as in the rest of my life, I really had no control over other people's rage. Even so, when they unleashed it all over me, I'd become indignant. I mean, wasn't I irreproachable? Their criticism was so unfair, so out of control. How could anyone be mad at me? Me!? The more I thought about it, the more I started to feel the corners of my mouth turning up.

Something about being completely exhausted gave me the strength to face an itty-bitty kernel of truth. People could be angry at me because people—including me—could be annoying. Or maybe people had their own issues that I, for some reason, triggered. But, all my life, no matter where the snarkiness came from, I personalized it. Anyone's less-than-glowing opinion of me was devastating, felt like personal rejection. I was amazed that morning, at nearly 59 years old, to realize finally that their rage may or may not—probably not, really—be my problem. I didn't have to absorb it and file it away as further proof of my own inadequacy and loserness. This was a revelation.

I laughed out loud.

"What's so funny, Pinto?" Shaun grinned from the starboard seat.

I grinned back at him. "Just enjoying a little personal growth this morning."

He nodded. He was probably doing the same – making an assessment of his life. Nothing else to do.

✦

Later, we powered 100 strokes to pass the 1299-mile mark–
halfway there! Team B emerged from the cabin to cheer and
celebrate with us. We popped the cork of a small bottle of tep-
id champagne, a gift from my dear friend Shauna, and passed
it around. Of course, we also kept rowing, powering 30s with
15-stroke breaks in between. The power strokes were enormously gratifying and empowering, but Ben was right. That
level of effort just wasn't sustainable, and we didn't want to
do any lasting damage. But we were past the halfway mark!
Almost there! HA.

Of course, Jonathan wasn't so much into the hard work.
He just wasn't. He was always late for his shift and seemed to
have no interest in actually rowing. Finally, Simon had had
enough.

"What the fuck, Jonathan?" Simon called from the bow.
"I'm really curious here. Why did you join this crew in the first
place? Please just tell me."

In the stern, Jonathan was working his jaw, silent.

"Because it obviously had nothing to do with winning,"
Simon went on. "Did you think it was going to be easy?" I
hadn't seen him this mad since Porto Moran. I couldn't decide
if I was into this or extremely uncomfortable. Maybe both.
"You really are the most selfish, most narcissistic–"

"Fuck off, Simon." Jonathan imitated Simon's posture,
mocking him.

No way. We were aghast. Mocking the captain?

Simon didn't miss a beat. "Get the fuck out of my sight.
Go back to your cabin. Now. Beth, take Jonathan's seat."

Jonathan didn't move.

"You're openly defying me. Is that it?" Simon cracked his
knuckles. "For once, you're *not* trying to get out of rowing?" I
worried his head was going to blow off. But then he stepped

back.

"Okay. You want a democracy?" He turned to Ben in the stroke seat. "What do you think, then? He stays or goes?" He looked so tired.

Ben knew exactly what to say. "I'd like him to stay right there and actually pull an oar."

If this was mutiny, at least it had the desired effect. Jonathan rowed without complaining for two solid hours. Sometimes anger works miracles.

Day 22

Ah, anger. I've been thinking about how I might unconsciously exaggerate what I receive from other people, use what I worry might be their anger to pierce my own heart. I wonder if I drive people away with my own panic. Do I internally focus on "How can you be so mean to me?" Like I'm the victim?

I'm sure I do it with Mike — He only shows he is angry with me if I am angry or annoyed with him. It's a defensive thing. But what if we could all talk about painful stuff without me falling apart? What if I could not assume the worst, not be crushed by some kind of implied criticism? Could I be open to it? Can I accept not being perfect? I'm actually starting to feel like maybe I can. What is this race doing to me?

On the positive side, a real live wash!!! Dan was generous enough to lend me a capful of soap. I washed my hair and body in a bit of water. It was glorious. Then another deep and wonderful sleep.

W4 WEDNESDAY

8-10 a.m. watch, caught the flash of a marlin's fin slicing the water like a sword. A school of shimmering dorado followed the boat just below the surface. Rowing was a slog that cloudy morning, the sea passive, with small grey and black tipped waves like ermine pelt. Averaged about five or six knots.

Boils, butt rash, BO, bad food, bad breath, saturated feet, gas, sore muscles, sore calves, sore asses. Mueslix, on the other hand–yum.

Ten naked men and their penises were just so not exciting. Ah, the cock sock–apparently an ocean rowing phenomenon–implemented to avoid sunburn.

"I asked my girlfriend for one for my voyage," Simon told us. Then he whipped out a teeny baby sock and moaned. "So this is what she thinks of me."

One of the guys lent him a normal sock.

Day 23

Cantaloupe sunrises and marlin strikes, we row hard and I live in my head. We are praying for landing before my March 4 birthday weekend, but it's no sure thing. Want everyone in my family and friends to show up in Barbados, but I can understand if no one can come since it is so much later than we anticipated. All is okay.

Lots of nice messages from Mike. Makes me homesick. I am tired.

W4 THURSDAY

Good watch! We did 15 knots and played flying fish poker.

Here's how it worked. The insane and self-destructive fish would leap out of the water and across the boat, smashing everyone and everywhere and performing aerial acrobatics. The rules of the game were that each person rotated choosing the next fish landing spot. Arbitrary and mad points were assigned for the fish that did the most deranged thing: 1000 points for a fish that actually smashed off the cabin and landed in a shoe, 500 points for a "self-cleaning" fish, one that slid back into the ocean so none of us had to touch it. These freaky fish were nauseatingly smelly and sticky, but so gorgeous. One landed on deck with wings splayed, so intricate and exquisite up close, like a giant stinking dragonfly.

We'd been 24 days at sea. Despite the hilarity of the poker game — bordering on maniacal, if you ask me — I started to wonder if I could actually take another week of this. Two weeks? I was sure I wasn't alone in that uneasiness. I wasn't sure I had a lot left to give.

I didn't dare whine, though. Guy had been dealing with the most serious onslaught of boils, all over his body. He had wounds everywhere and seeping sores- a good thirty-plus boils. He must have been miserable, but he maintained his dignity and still came out to row.

Even Colin was starting to show signs of extreme fatigue. Colin, who approached everything and everyone with warm equanimity. Colin who, at one point during a shift change, crawled past me then stopped, astonished, and murmured, "You! You're rowing with earrings on." Even sweet Colin lost his temper, and it cast a pall on us all. He was angry and in despair, threw something down as he stalked off to the men's cabin. Colin's fury marked a new low in morale. I just tried not to think too much.

Then Jen blamed me for why she couldn't sleep. Apparently, I had "too much stuff" in the cabin. Pretty crazy, since my one small yellow bag didn't take up much space. I didn't mind that she wore my sneakers to row when I was off shift. I did mind when she spilled the "community" shampoo into the ocean. Remember when she guaranteed us all that she'd have enough to last the whole trip? Well, oh well. It actually felt pretty good not to take her accusations too seriously. Was this the new me?

Birds were chasing the flying fish. The poor fish would skim over the waves like antelopes on the prairie, with birds in hot pursuit. Extraordinary to witness.

Day 24

Morning: jumping Bonito Dorado are back. Mueslix. Slept hard in the am. Talked to Mike and Regan on the SAT phone. I miss them. I had to sleep in the coffin as we are trying to take turns to spare still disabled Roger the agony. I was trying to sleep but it is so filthy in the coffin and so claustrophobic. Beef Bolognaise for dinner.

W4 FRIDAY

Delicious, glorious sleep. We inventoried our food and drink and snack packs, and we had only just enough if we were careful. We needed to get there sooner than later. Starving was not part of the plan.

The night before, a 47-meter tanker, *The Alter Ego*, called us on the radio. "What are you, a rowing boot?"

"No," answered Simon. "We're a rowing booooat," (emphasis on the long "o").

"Och, my GOD," they rattled back, clearly astonished at

little us in the big big sea. We shared reports of the oncoming weather. They told us to anticipate 20-knot winds! Hurray. I was having pretty severe sciatic problems in my left leg, so anything that could move us along faster was most welcome.

The fish danced in the waves, flamboyant, over the top. Who was in charge of the art design here? Too much.

Day 25

My daughter was accepted to Harvard (and Brown and BC). What a triumph.

Afternoon shift HOT, still seas, slow row. We hung a scarf over the hatch to try to give some shade to the cabin. The waves are relentless.

W4 SATURDAY

Tired, little sleep all yesterday. Bad sciatica. It was so hot and very slow. No winds materialized. 5.6 knots in two hours.

I should have been ready for it when Anna started handing out pronouncements.

"Put your bag away," she demanded. "It's in everybody's way."

I looked around the cabin. My tiny bag, which I used for a pillow, was in no one's way. Even if it had been, I think I would have resisted her self-appointed authority. Why did she and Jen feel like they were in a position to give everyone else orders? I would have preferred a discussion. I might have been more willing to comply with their misplaced needs if they'd been nicer about it. "I'll do it next shift," I growled.

"Do it now," Jen jumped in, hands on hips like a scoldy schoolmarm. "It's always in the way. Simon said it, too."

"What are you talking about?" That familiar feeling of anger, my own and theirs, so debilitating–I could feel my neck warming up. "You talked to Simon about me? About how to take up space in our cabin?"

"So what if I did? We talk about a lot of things." Was that a little smile in the corner of her mouth? How infuriating.

"I'm going to sleep," I sighed. "Let's have some quiet time." I puffed my bag lovingly and set my head down on it.

First thing in the morning, Simon came in, his ever-loving cheerful self, to chide us for not being team players and for not putting our bags away. He explained ever so patiently that since he and occasionally Colin were staying in our cabin on their off shifts, it would be helpful if we all put our bags away. My instinct to please the boss nearly surpassed any fight I had left in me, but I had to ask.

"Are you here because Jen whined about my bag?" I couldn't stand the thought that she was dictating my behavior through him. Could we not talk about the problem instead? Amongst ourselves? Without the master and commander here to lay down the last word? "All due respect, Simon, I don't think we need you here to referee."

"Just put the bags away." He looked around. "All of you."

I was furious, probably well beyond the limits of reason. But, as we worked together to get everything stashed, I also felt something lifting. People behave unjustly. People can get angry, act stupid, be cruel, perhaps – okay, definitely – including myself. It is also clear that in a contained environment like this, petty things become the object of contention and control. I could choose to receive the negativity or not. I was ashamed to have acted like a petulant child, but we all had.

At any rate, we put it all away.

✦

Guy taught me a "tapping intervention" for the sciatica. He explained about tapping at different pressure points on the body as a self-care technique designed to relieve negative emotions. "Just tap this spot with your fingertips and say, 'I forgive and accept myself.'"

I was ready to try anything, so I tapped. "Even though my ass is killing me," I started, "I forgive and accept myself." I felt silly. I tapped and chanted.

Remarkably, after a few rounds, my angry mood lifted, and I fell into a deep sleep. Halfway through, I woke to a severe burning sensation consuming my left leg, but tapped again and repeated, "I forgive and accept myself." Back to sleep. I was unsure what I was forgiving myself for, perhaps the betrayal of my body? Maybe it was more about whatever you have done or thought, you have to accept yourself.

Is pain really so much in our minds?

✦

Later that day, we took a swim. The sun was so hot and the Atlantic, calm and cool. We were feeling some resistance from the hull, so we jumped in the water to scrape barnacles. Very refreshing. A school of playful dorado, iridescent with clown bright faces, seemed to want to come in close and check us out. We loved the dorado because when they were present, sharks weren't. They were our watch dogs, making it safe for us to swim in the ocean. Shaun took photos of the fish and of us waving as we abandoned ship and swam off.

It was a peculiar thing, for this *Brittania III*, our tiny blob, to be our only lifeline in this aqueous world. I felt quite vulnerable swimming out there, 1000 miles from shore. Everyone else did, too. Funny, how sometimes with adversity comes conviviality.

Our waterline was so much higher now that we had eaten

most of the food, I was afraid I would not be able to get back in the boat. Evidently, however, we had all gotten a lot stronger, and even I was able to bench press myself back in with relative ease.

That afternoon, a big storm came up from the southwest, a 16-knot wind against us. It made for a hard pull; we had been making 1.7 knots rowing in unison in the calm, but suddenly we were slipping south in the wind. We didn't want to slip south. There was a danger of missing our destination altogether.

Day 26

I was going to call my son but the weather was not conducive to making a phone call.

Text from Mike. Ship of Fools: a 15th Century novel about a group of crazy townspeople who go to sea with no captain and no destination. It hits close to home.

Suffer Fools Lightly — be kind to fools. Okay.

W4 SUNDAY

Night shift, watched the squall come across the sea, an ominous black cloud with tendrils of dark rain racing toward us, then surrounding, attacking. Brutal 15-knot winds pushed us backwards, we flailed in the wild chaos. Then it passed, a memory.

I calculated: If we arrived on time, I would only have to do six more late-night watches and six more midnight watches. Fun to think about, but at this rate, it wasn't going to happen like that. We were behind schedule, and my boils were record-breaking. I started on the amoxicillin like the rest of the crew, treating these demons with what few antibiotics we had on board. But so tired. So done.

W4 MONDAY

Last night was at least a pleasant and harmonious watch. I was surprised. For winning the 2000-mile mark, we tipped back our two capfuls of awful rum and Dan's special hot chocolate. This Breakfast Club did score when we had to – we ALWAYS pulled together to hit the milestones. 2000 miles – we were awesome and strong.

But feelings on the watch can flip like a switch. Our later shift up was discouraging, slow and very hot. I'd woken up with an extreme migraine, a fist gripping my brain so torturously I could not eat lunch. My body was breaking down. Twenty-eight days at sea and the swell was heading south. 4-5 knot breeze, 1.5 knot current. Shit.

Day 28

We talked about what we would do immediately and then long term upon arrival. In my personal rowing musings, I constructed a list:

1. do garden and water feature
2. insulate the porch and put in windows
3. Mexico — canaries, roof garden a la Canary Islands
4. be a better friend
5. spend time with my son
6. diving? Boat?
7. Triathlon

Seems dumb and simplistic, but feels so good to focus on home.

11

Week Five

In Like a Lion

Well. That was February. A whole month at sea, each day swallowed by the sameness of the next.

A ship passed at night, a Nigerian tanker, Moran Penelope. They were all so beautiful and silent, those ghost ships that glided out of the night, ultimate stealth until they were almost upon us, a mountain of a beast. Although freighters are considered a big risk for ocean rowing, they (and we) were equipped with GPS and SAT phones. We had nothing to fear.

But things were definitely starting to get ugly. I figured that my body had a thirty-three-day warranty, but the contract was wrapping up and the body was quitting. I had tendonitis bad, a pinched nerve in my shoulder, an infected finger, lingering headaches, and boils so evil they could bring the devil himself to tears. Now would definitely be the time to call in the reserves: my innate cheerfulness just had to lock in. Maybe I would have to simply "act as if"? Remember that stuff about not thinking? Or maybe I should focus on taking care of everyone else? Sometimes that helped.

Nabs was contacted by a reporter regarding rioting in his hometown of Oman. He must have been worried. I tended to the boil on Dan's hip, a good three-four inches in diameter, infected and penetrating deep under layers of skin. I cleaned and bandaged it, then gave him some of the precious remaining antibiotics. He was clearly in terrible pain. Simon, the idiot, had squeezed the boil on his elbow to great infectiousness. I made him bare it to me so I could disinfect and wrap it, but he kept squeezing it anyway. Didn't he know it was not a pimple? The danger of sepsis was real and close at hand.

The Moran Penelope had given a discouraging report of weather, but when the wind picked up, we were doing high three- and low four-knots. The sea was choppy (ouch, when the wave caught your oar and bashed it into your body), and rowing was tough but fast.

Shaun, such a sweetheart, took my turn in the coffin, a disgusting claustrophobic hole I abhorred. It was filled with skin flakes and bits of old food. Plus, every time someone entered the cabin, they had to step over your face, dangling their huge asses and hanging packages and...aromas. Enough was enough. Shaun was such a good boy.

Shared Katmandu Curry with Roger for lunch – it was one of our favorites.

Day 29

Most everyone has lost or broken their "sporks" and are now forced to eat with their hands or squeeze the food bags from the bottom and eat the food as it squelches up. It was so demeaning and gross that everyone felt demoralized. I feel lucky to be able to tape a tongue depressor as a handle for my broken spork and still use it to eat. We share the "utensil" between all of us and use it to mix the hot water with the dry food. In the end, there is a survivor mentality of sharing.

Dear Lord. The boat is leaking into the Hendersons from below. Simon, of all of us, is unfazed. A third of the food ruined. The rest of us are worried. I suspect the water came in where the hull was repaired back in La Gomera. God, that was a long time ago.

W5 WEDNESDAY

We did 75 knots in 24 hours. The currents and wind were finally in our favor! Hooray! Mueslix for breakfast was always a gift.

A significant squall approach from the east, smacked us down and then moved on. We were a teeny-weeny speck of nothing in the middle of the big blue sea. All soaked and smelly – the men in particular, but really all of us – gas and BO and putrid bodies. As if you couldn't find the dead hamster you lost in your dirty laundry a week ago. Put a piece of bandage around my thigh as a way to protect my boil.

We had started rationing food because, between spoilage from leaking hatches and our being at sea longer than we anticipated, we just didn't have enough to last another week (or more). From the required 8000 calories a day, we were down to around 3000. To get there, we had to substitute desserts for real food. This might sound awesome to some, and it's not that I loved the inevitable chili con carne, beef bolognaise, chicken and vegetable pasta, and much-coveted shepherd's pie, but I hated the remaining desserts. The best ones had been gobbled up long before. Rice pudding and sultanas or custard and various fruit pieces or "chocolate chip dessert"? These were "vegetable-fat-infused milk products," high in calories, very low in delectability. They tasted like something burned in the oven.

Snack packs were doled out at midnight on alternate days – no more nightly treats. The best was a chocolatey energy drink, Peronin, which was high in calories and vitamins and tasted pretty great as a drink, especially warm. These, we relished.

Roger was doing a great deal of singing. He sang about everything. I know it was his way of wiling away the hours, and his soothing songs were a panacea for the soul. Roger was a self-contained man who was suffering now from various ailments, but he was also a very good man who cared about all of us. We took turns in the despised coffin.

Beth was less of a team player. As a psychologist, I would have labeled her narcissistic and try to validate her feelings. As a teammate, I just got bored with her endlessly fascinating favorite topic – herself – and her laziness, working the oar about half the time during every shift. Still, it felt good not to get pissed off or even care that much, and just to be able to let it go.

Was this progress? Or deterioration?

Shaun spent some time explaining British vocabulary to me.

Mankie: gross.

Whinging: whining.

Gringer: disgusting person.

Day 30

Today I keep searching my mind for my mother and I cannot find her. I have realized I have created a delusion, that if I do everything in my power to make myself perfect, then no one can ever find fault and be angry and leave me. So when someone is angry it has been perplexing and unjust and fearful. A confirmation of lack of worth. So now that I am realizing this···what next?

Both iPods are dead. I want to kill Jonathan. And Beth. And everyone. We're all getting on each other's nerves. Not surprising. We are all deteriorating.

I know it's a survival tactic, thinking about what's next. Can I make it all happen? Yeah, I think I can.

W5 THURSDAY

Well, one of the worst things that could happen finally happened.

It was at the end of a long watch. We suddenly lost control of the boat and were slip-sliding this way and that. OH NO. The automatic steering pilot had broken. The system used sensors, a course computer (like a GPS) and a drive unit to steer the boat. A virtual helmsman. The autopilot helped us maintain our desired heading and our route while at the same time compensating for wind and current to stay on course. We'd spent the whole journey on auto-pilot. It was an essential component of the race.

What were we supposed to do? Hand steering the rudder was back breaking and inefficient. We'd be sliding all over the sea. Moment of panic. The swells were large and beautiful, but we were zigzagging like crazy. Nabs was trying to hand-steer by compass. Simon worked on it all morning. At one point, he asked if any of us had chewing gum, so I dug up some salty old sticks from the bottom of my bag, chewed them up, and handed them over. Turns out he used them for insulation. Pretty resourceful guy, I guess.

At least I still had my spork. It was an amazing truth, how much I'd come to value something so otherwise meaningless. A spork in this situation was gold, like milk for your Mueslix or a working iPod. Both of which had illuminated the Buddhist teaching that everything is temporary.

When Jen's jacket was blown overboard, she borrowed mine. Fine. But I had left my makeshift tongue depressor spork in the pocket. Curse me, lack of foresight! When I got my jacket back that morning, the spork was crushed. Mine was one of the last sporks aboard, and I believe we all felt the blow.

I was aggrieved. Vegetable shepherd's pie out of the pack with my fingers—happy birthday eve to me.

Day 31

Why did I do this and waste 3 months of my life? Looks like we will not get to shore for twelve more days. It feels like a constantly receding rainbow.

Shaun, though, is total sweetness. He lent me his iPod. Made everything okay.

Tomorrow's my birthday. 59. Have I done a good job so far? Have I fulfilled my agreement with myself and the crew? Have I pulled my own weight?

W5 FRIDAY

Night shift and the steering broke again. Those beautiful swells that could have pushed us ahead, given us something to surf on, we couldn't catch. We were trying desperately to keep from turning broadside to the waves. We lost ground.

On the other hand, it was pretty cool to be steering by the sun and stars. Apparently, those long classes in England on celestial navigation came in handy after all. Simon bolted an oar to the rudder so we could hand-steer from the outside.

It was the last day of my 59th year, and melancholy was the word of the day. After watch, I crawled into the cabin with a heavy heart and planted my face in the pillow for a good silent cry.

Then I felt Shaun's hand gentle on my foot. "You want to talk about it?"

Sometimes other people's big hearts, their kindness, that's what puts me over the edge. I lost it so many times with my dad, when he'd step right up to my trembling chin and ask, "You okay, Suzy?" What is it about other people's care that opens up the floodgates?

I cried. What was I supposed to tell him, though? I knew the tears were much more about exhaustion than about anyone's bad behavior or my dead iPod or the stabbing pain in my shoulder, though that last one was definitely no fun.

We decided the best idea might be to clearly enumerate our complaints.

"I can't believe those idiots wrecked my iPod," I moaned.

"I'm so hungry I could eat a flying fish," he fake sobbed.

"I hate dessert!" This one started out as a wail, but ended in a giggle.

Shaun was trying unsuccessfully to keep the corners of his mouth down. "This cabin smells like balls and farts and lady parts!"

Of course, it took about thirty seconds before we were both cracking up – almost literally hysterically – and then I couldn't decide whether this was the best or the worst birthday of my life.

When the next shift started, Simon graciously offered a birthday strip-o-gram, which I declined only because we'd all seen quite enough of the boys, thanks very much. I took a sweet hug instead. Anna and Colin made a cake using an old dish mold. They'd collected slapjack bars and chocolate for a week from crew snack bags, a grand sacrifice from all since we are now down to 1500 calories a day.

Raspberry Crumble Cake Recipe
1. Take crumbled slapjack candy
2. Pour over all melted chocolate
3. Empty a raspberry crumbles package as the third layer
4. Use M&M's to spell out "39-ish" (aw, Nabs!)

We each got two bites. Everyone sang. I felt a special gratitude for the party planners who gave me a birthday on a shoestring. Okay, on an oar...string?

Then a huge squid got swept into the boat and was oozing around on deck. Big night for flying fish, too. One flew right into Guy's shoe, hanging on the line: 10,000 points!

Back in the cabin, written all over the walls:

From Simon, "Happy Birthday Suzanne."

Anna: "Suzanne I miss you. For me the worst thing about the trip is that we're on opposite watches. You are the best. Lots of love."

Jen: "Wishing you well. You are an inspiration. Happy B'day."

Colin, after I gave him my Picnic bar: "Suzanne you are an inspiration and a fantastic teammate and a wonderful lady. Thank you."

Couldn't help but wonder if the whole crew – and the rest of the universe – were conspiring to make this birthday extra special. More than special. Lifesaving.

Day 32

I am fearful of talking to my family today as I just might cry. So homesick. 59 years old today. I had not planned on being here for my birthday.

When I left on January 1 I had no idea I would be gone almost 3 months. So yesterday was feeling sad and despairing and worried and homesick. Especially since the closer we get the more days we get tacked on.

Every day I hurt in new ways as does the rest of the crew and poop buckets jump ship, spork and 2 IPODS crash, the steering is gone. I am not alone I know, and most of us clench our teeth and button our lips.

On the other hand, with boils and burned-out bums and bad food and bad odors and lousy accommodations, where else other than in the frickin' nowhere of the Atlantic would it be cooler to spend a birthday? I am honored and privileged to do this adventure with everyone.

Talked to Mike and Regan. Regan said she will be in the Bahamas on March 14-16 to meet us. Shit — Wouldn't that be terrible if she and Cindy came all that way and had to leave before we showed up? Not sure what the deal is with Mike. He had originally protested there was no need for him to meet me, and I had been trying to adjust to that fact all trip. Now he seems to be changing his mind.

Text from my son— He and his girlfriend will be there. He is excited. I am more so. The message from him stated he is so proud and excited and telling everyone.

Okay then. Everyone will be there on March 14-16 so I had better be there too. I am sustained by their love and their faith in me. We got this. I have to ask Regan to bring a movie camera and sharpies to sign oars: ROW HARDER.

W5 SATURDAY

We had run out of everything: antibiotics, bandages, fresh wipes etc. Everyone was covered with boils, especially on the backs of their legs and butts. You'd crawl out to your shift and try to sit, but the pain was gruesome. You had no choice. Then the endorphins set in and you went numb. You rowed and rowed and rowed. At the end of the shift, you crawled back to your cabin and couldn't sleep because of the thrumming pain.

Blood everywhere. We rinsed our sheepskin seat covers in the sea and hung them from the center line, hoping they would dry by the next shift. In the meantime, at shift change, we all had to crawl down the center line to our cabins with the reeking sheepskins hitting us in the face. It was the march of the dead monkeys.

We were, finally and truly, falling apart. Seeing only ocean for infinite miles in every direction, not punctuated by anything, was utterly disorienting. Prisoners in solitary describe numbness, the loss of hope that's been called a "murder of the soul."

I could not rest because of the pain.

Guy was in even worse shape, with new boils popping up everywhere. Fevered and lethargic, this man still took his shifts and rowed as best he could. I learned he was sleeping in his foulies so as not to contaminate everyone. The thought of that was unbearable, so I gave him my silk liner with a reprimand to get out of the foulies. They were absolutely Hazmat. I could rest a little better knowing that sleeping in the silk liner would be a bit of a relief for him.

Shaun and Roger, too, broken. Ben had become quiet, passive aggressive, given to moodiness. Jonathan and Beth had a different drama for every shift. All in pain, covered with infected boils, shattered. All still rowing.

That morning, a roar erupted outside, grizzly and gnarly. I heard one oar hit another, a sure sign that something was coming apart at the seams.

"Argh!" Mike was shouting, "me aching joints! I can't keep this up for much longer!" He seemed desperate, almost panicked. Here was this stalwart meat-and-potatoes fireman giving in to the pain. Almost.

Another oar crack. In his efforts to row hard, Mike was gripping the oar too tightly. He'd developed severe tendonitis in his fingers and his hands were permanently clawed.

"Mike!" many of us called at once.

"How can we help?" I asked from the cabin.

He was silent then, back and forth. I couldn't see his face, but I could tell by the shape of his shoulders that he was probably fighting tears. "It's my family," he finally granted quietly, "they need me. I can't even remember what the hell I am doing here." Catch, drive, return.

We tried to comfort him, but I knew it wouldn't work. He shrugged us off.

Day 33

Mandatory 2nd shift. 4 hours, we rowed twelve knots. My shift just cooked it, rowing hard, almost in unison, coasting the waves, making musical time. How can there be so much pain and so much power, all at once?

Two things I know for sure:

I haven't learned acceptance of things out of my control after all

People are good.

Brushed hair and changed bandages and made a new spork. 8-10 days out, we think and hope. How lovely for me: coming to meet me are my best friend, best sister, best kids, all coming.

Remember when we thought we'd be done in 33 days?

About 600 miles left today. 9 more days. Please.

W5 SUNDAY

5.3 to 5.6 knots. Following seas, the stars bountiful and the air soft.

We lost our last Home Depot poop bucket overboard, so we sawed the top off a plastic jug. But sitting on the rough edge was more than anyone could bear, so we were glad when that, too, was washed away by a wave. Then Mike developed a new system. We'd use the rigger for a toilet.

We should have been doing this all along. We'd hang our asses through the rigger, bouncing up and down with the boat, and let it fly. Somehow, this created an amazingly weird vacuum sensation, sort of like an inverse bidet. Your business all disappears. Maybe it was a little scary in a heavy sea and you'd have to be lashed in at night so as not to be swept overboard, but we loved it.

As the appointed "medic," I'd been hoarding sparse supplies to give to those in most need. So when Dan joined the ranks of those desperately suffering with boils and a giant wound on his hip, I sent him medication, bandages, and tape with a note to guard it with his life against those who would steal it. This is what we had come to.

We wondered if someone had absconded with all of the tissue paper packets since Beth had quite a few left but there were none available to the rest of us. We had to ration our fresh wipes we used as toilet paper. Odd that so much had gone missing.

Dan was in charge of navigating and cooking. The Popular Kids shift was sharing that responsibility, but Dan was so devastated by large boils (six inches in diameter and several skin layers deep) that he simply couldn't row. He was hurt and unhappy.

Dan was great with the fun facts. For example, he filled us in about flying fish. They stink. The slime that covers them is actually a layer of mucus designed to protect them from parasites. This layer supposedly makes them more aerodynamic, though my guess is that their balletic maneuvering is more about their pectoral "wings" and a crazy forked tail that propels them so far out of the water. Again, Dan told us that the Navy tried to synthetically recreate the viscous substance to paint on their battleships for ballistics protection, fire suppression, and other uses. He insisted this was actual fact. We were entertained.

It was also Dan who sent me the most precious gift of an REI titanium spork. So weird, and so nice! What an offering – it was ridiculously special to me. I shared it with the "cook" for stirring and with my crew, all of us taking turns to eat in a civilized manner with an actual utensil. Lucky us, and what a dear thing for Dan to do. I didn't even try to remember a time when we could all take utensils for granted.

Day 34

The dorado and marlin are jumping, a skyward dance.
I learned they are slapping onto the water to get rid
of parasites.

Roger- we cheered him for having 100 days at sea
under his belt. I wrote him a wall note.

My bathing suit strap broke.

The boil is better.

Called Mike and told him I want to come to Mexico post
row. Then we can drive to Colorado with my dogs, Gi-
tana and Sonora. In mid-April, we'll go to Portugal for
Mike's business trip. We will see how things turn out.

The Brittania III is going to arrive March 14 or 15.
Saturday or Sunday I think. Today is Sunday. Just one
more week. I almost can't take it.

I have so much to do. To distract myself, I'm making
plans. No rhyme or reason, just whatever pops in my
head:

1. meet with PO officers

2. dinner with Co-worker

3. progress reports

4. pick up more evaluations

5. take some social workers to lunch by way of apology

6. apology re: conference I will not be there to speak at

7. low-cost evaluations on abused kids and abusive parents

Plans for Mexico:

1. Garden in bedroom

2. Bring home Canaries to brighten the mornings with song a la Canary Islands

3. Bring saddle, bridle, scuba equipment, boat to Mexico

4. Money to my daughter-in-law. I owe her

5. Begin training for upcoming triathlon

6. Call my friends with love and enthusiasm

7. Write Wellesley magazine to check if they want an article on this trip

8. Write to Boulder Community Rowing —need happy hour with my team

9. Write/call brother John: I want to see him, it has been too long

10. Give up Boulder office

7:30 pm watch 538 — 7.5 miles to 520.0

2:00 watch 543 ending 537 — 6 miles

W5 MONDAY

- 2-6 watch, eleven miles. We passed the 500-miles-to-go mark, made it to 493. Beth rowed one stroke.

- 8:30-11 watch, six miles to 483.7. It was slow.

- 12-2 watch, six miles

- 5-7:30 watch, six-plus miles and now 459.5

- 10-2 watch, eight miles to 448

Because our stocks were running so low, Simon levied new food rationing. We were now down to about 800 calories a day, 1/10 of the race guidelines for calorie intake.

Rice pudding for breakfast. I hated rice pudding, but we only got two main meals today. Tomorrow, they told us, we'd have breakfast, a pudding and snack pack, and only one main meal. Other than my chocolate bar, I gave my snack pack to Shaun. He is so skinny, still growing, and such a hard, consistent, and uncomplaining rower.

It was very very warm and hothouse steamy now in the cabins. Breathless. If you lay very very still, you could almost feel a breeze. I enjoyed a wonderful 2.5 hours of sleep until the haunting of a bad anxiety/guilt dream about my failure to care for others. The men were distraught and enraged at the heat. The mood was…ornery.

"Hey, Dan," I offered helpfully, "want some help with the cooking?" I knew he was navigating, but I was hungry—we all were—and he was the cook.

He looked at me, then back down at the maps. Ah. The silent treatment.

"Hey, Pinto," Ben chimed in, "how about let the guy do one thing at a time?"

Ouch.

I moved Simon's stuff off my seat so I could sit down to row.

"Oh sorry," he barked. "Was my stuff in your way? Next time, I'll be sure to stash it properly."

So mean. We were turning into *Lord of the Flies*. I laughed at my own righteous indignation. Me? Do wrong? How dare they chide me! Then the tears came. I hadn't changed much after all, but at least I could step back and observe my oversensitive response and immediate punitive silence. Could we call that progress?

The dorados, surfing beside us beneath the waves, were encased in blue amber, translucent blades running up the swells and breaking free on the other side. Through my polarized sunglasses, totally transfixing. Several man o' war bonnets also puffed by, bubblegum pink soldiers marching through the water, a whole cavalcade. We played "Count the Fish Jumps," port vs. starboard. Starboard won by a mile.

Simon announced that his weather forecaster, Passage Weather, was predicting complete calm for forty hours, which means we were going nowhere slowly. The water was sluggish. We'd hit the doldrums.

On the bright side, it meant that tomorrow morning we'd be so becalmed that we could swim.

Day 35

An exciting announcement! Tomorrow is "wash" day. We start gathering extra fresh water in from the desalinator to share a couple of buckets for the whole crew. Fresh water at all is, well, so refreshing. Most of us use our allotment of water to pour over wounds/ boils. Washing now is interesting as Jen refuses to share any soap after Beth spilled some of the bottle.

Now Jen and Anna get to use soap and Beth and I are without.

12

Week Six

Land HO!

- 6-8:30 watch, six miles to 429
- 11-1 shift, six miles down to 417
- 3-5 shift, six miles to 408
- 7:30 -10 watch, seven miles to 393

We need to do 66 miles per day.

Day 36

Mueslix for breakfast, chili con carne for lunch. Such

abundance.

We swam today! And bathed! Just rinsing with fresh water because no soap. I tried to shave my legs but they would not shave. Seriously, the hair is so long and hard and pulverized with salt the razor could not shave them. Lot of men o' wars. The water was brisk but lovely and a little scary when the dorados weren't there. It is shocking how fast the boat was going at 1.5 knots without our rowing. We had to swim to keep up.

More boils. Received word from Jen's doctor that the bacteria we all have been afflicted with is contagious. Duh.

Staying in our current lineup for another day but it hurts. It relieves some of the tendonitis that afflicts all of our joints by changing sides.

We only have six drink packs for 6 days divided between Peronins and B-lodas on alternate days.

Flying fish head smack.

W6 WEDNESDAY

- 2-6 shift, 12 miles to 367 and the sunrise was…uplifting

- 8:30-11 shift, six miles to 353.9

- 1-3 shift 5.5 miles to 343.5

- 6.5 miles down to 331

- 10 miles down to 319

Shaun's question: Why is the sea blue? Anna wrote the answer with a diagram on the wall of the cabin: red and green light are absorbed. Salt water absorbs greater red and green and there is more blue light around anyway so the sea reflects the sky. She was brilliant.

Simon lent me his iPod. I didn't know most of the music, but some of it came across loud and clear. The band America's "Horse with No Name" nailed it: "the ocean is a desert with its life underground and a perfect disguise above." Exactly.

When the frigate birds appeared in the sky, we let out a cheer. They cannot land on water or fly over 500 miles. We were approaching land!

No more whining. Instead, we imagined Geoff and Don Allum, cousins who rowed the Atlantic in a double in long-ago times, 1971. They ultimately had no more than a half cup of water a day to share and minimal food left. Don died from complications later. We met Geoff in La Gomera as he came to see us off.

So, we ate our one main meal a day and shared pudding with some measure of gratitude. There was only one more breakfast left and one more day with two meals for each of us. And we were moving slowly.

Dan ate a flying fish. We tasted it: rank. This was the new austerity. We shared a Raspberry Crumble and no Peronin. No night meals.

Day 37

Very tumultuous sea. Wind is ten knots NE and sea running due south. Stunning resplendent sunsets and clouds but every stroke is a battle to maintain our course.

I am having nightmares about being a galley slave and Shaun is a pirate who forced me to row and I wake weeping that I don't want to plus he was going to read my journal out loud to the crew. I just wept.

Other nightmares of neglecting my loved ones. I guess the anxiety is growing.

Called Mike — not there

Talked to my daughter

Heard from Mike's son: wonderful

Washed some garments

Resented of the number of breaks Beth took.

Recognized some common ground between the "I'm irreproachable" syndrome and my expectations of others. Huh.

Plan: Write to Backpacker's Pantry about how much we love their food and to Smartwool about their wonderful socks and shirt.

W6 THURSDAY

- 11-1 watch, four miles done to 239. Beam wind, the sea was moving North to South. Very slow, very difficult.

- 2:30-5 watch, 4.6 miles to 280 to go. Found a chocolate bar.

The sea was still heavy, slow long swells to the south. These were gigantic walls marching on and on forever, and we were just caught in them, part of the parade. There was little breeze but some cloud cover, which helped.

Lamb Pilaf. Eating once a day made me feel bloated. It was very hot and sunny.

Jennifer, my rowing buddy and good friend in Colorado, insisted that "you are where you are supposed to be." But I was starting to really wonder. Was I supposed to be behind a large officious man without pants who periodically lifts a plump cheek to fart resoundingly in my direction?? This was where I was meant to be?

Six frigate birds dove and twirled around us in feats of aerial acrobatics.

Beth just couldn't row anymore. She was crying out of discouragement and it was totally understandable.

Simon noted I was one of the few who'd never missed a watch. No kidding, I thought. I just wanted to get there.

Day 37

Beautiful deep sleep with meds for pain. Shin splints and both ankles are swollen. Starting a new boil on my ankle. Right elbow has a pinched nerve to hand and fingers. Food down to Mueslix for breakfast and one meal (Beef Bolognaise) and shared Raspberry Crumble among crew for the day — 800 calories on the dot. We are hungry.

Still, we concluded our shift with a 2000-meter sprint. It was pretty cool and exciting. We all got jazzed to be racing and synchronized.

Interesting internal conversation with my Dad and baby

brother Chris where I felt I had to apologize for my condescension toward them while they were alive. I have discovered in many ways I could be as critical as my own mother, judgmental and internally, silently patronizing.

In falling asleep I was having some interesting thoughts about prayer. I suddenly got (duh) that you are supposed to have an ongoing relationship with God and thank him daily for all he gives you, etc. You are not supposed to ask for anything for yourself. I think I finally understood what Christians do — they have what they feel is a relationship. Perhaps in the context of the relationship you can slip in a request or two. This is something I cannot conjure up in my own belief system. Have I no faith?

It is very hard to each night be counting this as your last or next to last at sea···and then it never is.

Wonderful messages from Mike encouraging us to get back, updates on the pets and life, a taste of the real world.

W6 FRIDAY

- Late-night watch, 10-plus miles to 248
- 8:30-11 watch, six miles to 236
- 1-3 watch, 5.5 miles to 226.5
- Morning, to 209
- Afternoon, 10 miles to 192. Our shift again took us below the 200-mile mark. We had no more rewards other than the miles behind us.

So hot. Every once in a while, a small breeze from the north-east would whiffle by, tiny relief. The sea wrinkled with small waves, but no large swells to push us along. We all thought this might be the almost-last day, but at this rate – yesterday was only a 62-mile day – we were looking at the 15th. The Ides of March. No one was talking about the trades anymore.

We shared a rice pudding and a custard between seven people, so four bites for each person. I meant to save half of my lunch, curried beef, for dinner, but I was too hungry.

Last night, big fight. Dan, whose job was to steer and cook, drank a Peronin. Peronin was just for rowers. Jonathan took it upon himself to reprimand Dan, and this escalated into a screaming fuck you fight. Dan had a temper tantrum and, being provocative as usual, Jonathan felt he had to have the last word. The fact that Simon took Dan's side on this was symptomatic of some interesting shifts in alliances. I talked to Dan later and he was okay.

Beth, on her part, felt too tired to come out and row and stayed in the cabin.

Guy was one brave man. He was so badly hurt, but he just kept going.

It was kind of viscerally exciting when Simon finally laid out the plan of action. Twenty-four hours in advance, we would know the time of arrival. We would try for the northern approach. We'd continue our regular watches. When we got within eight miles, whether it was our watch or not, Shaun and I were to place ourselves so that we could be the first off the boat. Holding a world record, turns out, was good for something. Very cool.

Simon also took orders for the feast that was being organized to greet us. I requested steak and salad and fruit. Depending on what time we got in, we could have a drink and then a shower, then come back together later in the day or evening.

I wasn't sure. Maybe I wouldn't hurry back to celebrate with these folks. My family was going to be there, and all I wanted was to surround myself with them.

Day 38

Thinking of my deceased little brother, Chris, thoughts of us calling him Christobito and the Red Snapper when he was young. Vowed to ask the other family members if they remember.

I sheepishly attribute the small variable waves to brother Chris (superstitious I know, but why not indulge in good energy?). Thanked him and apologized for being such a lousy sister. I need to write to his widow, Susan, but on second thought that would be just to fill my own needs for expiation.

Gorgeous peaches and cream sunrise and a cerulean sky. It reminds me of my college roommate Pam's poster in college. Maxfield Parrish. She was the one who introduced me to art at all as I was woefully ignorant. Thanks, Pam.

W6 SATURDAY

- 6-8:30 watch, only 5 miles to 177. Big Skippy (as my Dad used to call God) frowned. Strong wind and big N-S swells.

- 11-1 watch, 5 miles to 166

Storm petrels cried in the face of a squall this morning. Portuguese men-of-war floated by with their gaudy roseate helmets, an army on the move. Large swells early, but then the weather changed.

That afternoon, we were slammed by tumultuous sea and big waves, half of which were hitting us broadside. It was crazy out there, hard rowing. Many times, I was swept right out of my seat and slammed into the cabin wall or the rigging, which hurt and was terrifying, as we scrabbled to hold on with clawed fingers, knowing our lives depended on it. It would totally suck to be swept overboard this close to the end.

We had taken to having a lottery to determine who got the good food. Boulder Backpacker's food was SO much better than anything else we had. The lottery was fun and funny, although there were genial disappointment and wild but unproductive bargaining when one didn't win the good stuff.

Two meals today–luxury!

Day 39

I am getting new boils all over my butt and legs. 4 new ones. My headache is gone with having food available. Message from Regan who was worried but excited.

Lesson: no matter how hard you try it doesn't matter— you won't get what you want.

I am sick of hauling everyone's lazy ass across this ocean. Jonathan actually took a shower during the row. WTF???

I realize it will take a while to figure out the good things about this experience.

I also realize from hearing about the other boats that if we'd left the Canary Islands when they did we would have gotten here right away. This is so discouraging I cannot sleep. Sent texts.

W6 SUNDAY

- 3-5 shift, 5.5 miles to 154.5

- 7:30 to 10 shift, 7.5 miles to 139. You could see – and smell – the squalls from far off, their curtains of rain sweeping toward us.

- 1:30 to 3:30, 11.5 miles to 121

- 6-9, 9.5 miles to 99.5! We made ourselves a Challenge, to go from a steady state to racing stroke rate of 33 per minute for the final 5 K for 3 miles in 45 minutes.

- 2-5, 7 miles to 75 miles to Barbados

Moving fast with the sea behind us. We were given full rations now. Not a good look, to come in as scarecrows. Beef Bolognese, Peronin, hot chocolate, and a snack pack. Cheese was all wet and rotted.

All that day, we watched the frigate birds. Then we saw an airplane vapor trail – the very first, much to Dan's boyish delight. In the middle of the Atlantic, the planes fly so high we never saw a vapor trail.

I was hit in the eye by a flying fish.

The rule is the first person to cry "Land Ho!" would have to buy drinks for all. The trick, we decided, was to get someone else to do it. Not sure if I'd be able to wait.

Day 41

I am in quite a bit of pain. I cannot sit. I finally got Mike the fireman to give me a plaster he was saving for my boils, and that was a great relief.

Squabbled with Beth. Ben played kindergarten teacher and intervened. Jonathan accused Roger of taking too much food. There is no place to withdraw from anyone and no place for a private conversation. We, Roger, Shaun, and I, wonder whether Beth appropriated some of the snack packs.

No cleaning up due to rough waves even though it is clean-up Thursday. I am disappointed I cannot clean up before seeing my family. Just looked at myself in video camera and I look very very old and fairly ugly. Will wear cap, have grey hair and my face is very old and very brown. Ugh. My hair is really silver. I should sleep but cannot. I am so so glad to be done. Internally I do feel triumphant.

Simon predicts Monday night. I am afraid to believe it.

W6 MONDAY

- (First watch), 10 miles to 57 to arrival
- 6-8:30 watch, 7 miles to 39 out
- 11-2 watch, 6 miles to 24 left to go

At 2 a.m., Simon cried "Land Ho!"

Barbados glowed in the distance. Good following sea, good wind.

During the late-night shift, a container ghost ship 14 miles away was headed straight toward us and did not see us. We could see her lights and hear a faint thrumming of engines. Very close. He asked if we were "the rowing ship." Nabs had him divert so as not to hit us.

The sea was moving at 1.2 knots. There was, however, a problem. Entering the harbor at night would be difficult and dangerous, laced with reefs and bounded by cliffs, and we didn't know if a boat would come out late to guide us in. If not, we would need to stop well before the sea pushed us in. No one wanted to stop. Simon promised to call it by midday.

A fancy Cessna circled overhead and we spoke by radio with the pilot, Dave. He was worried we needed assistance. Dave had been following our voyage on the internet, so he came out to take a look and to welcome us to Barbados. Seemed like people were actually noticing, even looking forward to, our arrival.

Regan texted: "Enough is enough. I'm swimming out to help."

Simon called it. We were heading in that night. We'd waited too long and would be pushed in anyway.

This seemed almost like the longest part of the journey, as we could make out the contours of land in the dusk, see cars and lights, smell the barbecues, but we were still so far from the port.

My team rowed beautifully in unison and did power strokes to bring us past the cement factory on the outer pier in the dark. But the centerboard was dragging on the reef and the steering was tricky. Waves crashed into the cliff walls. This was exactly where Roger lost his spot in the race before.

We finished our shift just as we got to the end of the factory wall and started to enter the port. Team B came on to row us in. Shaun and I stood in the bow looking for the designated landing spot, but it was pitch black. We could see nothing. It would be easy to go off course and miss the mooring area altogether. God only knows what we could run into out there.

BREEEEEAH! We sounded the air horn and lit a flare. We're here! Then, from far off to the left, a dull roar emanated out of the blackness. A jubilant signal from our waiting families. We returned with the horn over and over. BREEEEAH!

"Follow the roar!" I shouted.

The rowers pulled even harder.

✦

How can I explain the feeling of coming into port? As we got closer, I could hear everyone's voices, my children's standing out specifically like solos in a symphony.

"MAAAAA!"

Shaun and I looked at each other, crying and hugging. The youngest and the oldest. We lit all the flares so that the boat was like something out of *Apocalypse Now*. We were totally alight and cheering and screaming. Somehow, we managed to come into the dock exactly right.

My daughter leapt forward to catch the line.

Simon opened a bottle of champagne to shake and spray all over us.

"We made it," he wept, choking. "Shaun and Suzanne, as record holders, you are the first to get off."

As planned, we all pivoted toward his beaming, sunburned face.

"No, no, Captain Simon," I smiled. "Please. You first. We are proud and honored to row under you as our captain."

Simon's face crumpled with emotion and tears, and he hopped off.

Shaun and I followed. We staggered off the vessel and fell into waiting arms. Our limbs were shaky and unused to solid ground, and I nearly collapsed.

EVERYONE was there including Mike. My whole world. Everyone I loved and cherished. We'd made it — I'd made it — home.

✦

The hours after our landing passed in a blur so much catching up and hugging and answering so many questions. We had pre-ordered dinner – mine was steak and vegetables – real live fresh meat – and the wine was lovely, though dizzying. My family and friends crowded around, pleased and deeply relieved that I'd made it. Everyone seemed to be chattering at once.

How can I describe the shower at the hotel? A cascade of clean warmth, and SOAP! My daughter said we all smelled so bad, and the boat was even worse. I finally got to go to sleep, sated, a little dizzy, and totally safe. I love my friends and family so much, and I cannot convey my gratitude that they were all there.

The next day, we were met with a big surprise. We were all commanded to appear at the Barbados Port Authority for illegal entry at night without permission. We stood around for an hour, wine or beer in hand, strangely quiet, until our passports were stamped. The major concern for the authorities in Barbados was that we could be bringing some infectious disease into the country. At that point, we honestly believed there was no chance of that.

Over luncheon, we introduced our supporters to one another and allowed them to investigate the boat, which was to be shipped back to England (after a good powerwashing, I hoped). Each of us in the crew was awarded an oar, with a decal affixed to the blade that read *Brittania III*. We all signed all of the oars for each other in permanent ink. Even though I had to saw my oar in two near the collar to take it on the plane, it now hangs proudly in my dining room in Mexico, a tribute to this amazing journey.

Mike left to go back to Africa. Adjustment to normal life was grand, but I felt increasingly ill and was tormented by continued outbreaks of boils. One morning, I awoke for work with a high fever and literally could not walk. I crawled to the phone and then to the car, then drove myself to the emergency room. I had just started to receive reports from other crew members that they, too, were being hospitalized, plagued by Methicillin-resistant Staphylococcus aureus – MRSA – a terrible infection caused by a type of staph bacteria that's become antibiotic-resistant and very dangerous. Research online indicated that on average, within one year, 21.8% of MRSA patients in the hospital died as compared with 5% of non-MRSA patients. Those not in the hospital had it even worse. We were all in serious trouble. Indeed, one of the crew was told that, had we been out there much longer, we would not have been able to survive.

I was whisked off to an isolation ward. Other than medical staff, no one was allowed to visit. I was pumped with super antibiotics until the infection lessened. My crewmates were in the same boat: because the bacteria had entered our blood streams, we were all enfeebled and susceptible to all kinds of other health dangers. Later, we discovered I had infected Mike with a different strain of MRSA, but fortunately only on his skin. Still, he didn't like it much.

Publicity was booming and exciting. Many of us gave television interviews and presentations. I don't want to sound my own horn, but I am both shy and proud of what I have done. And I have loved sharing the adventure with others.

People ask me if, given the adversity, I would do it again. Invariably, the answer is YES. In fact, two years after completing the Woodvale Challenge, I was presented with the opportunity to cross the Pacific with the same crew. Now knowing what to expect, I thought, and with the opportunity to do it again *better*, more wisely and less selfishly, I tentatively agreed. All memories of danger and pain, the struggles with interpersonal relationships amongst the crew, fell by the wayside. I wanted to go because I was invigorated, because I believed I could do it. It was all pretty exciting until I was bombarded by my family and children with a chorus of resounding NOs. I didn't go, and it was probably the right move. These days, I have to confess that my body is probably a little too broken down to make the attempt. I could, no would, do it though.....

Why? This is the common question I hear. Why did I do it? And why in the world would I consider doing it again?

It is not often in life that one has the opportunity to do the hardest thing. The Woodvale Challenge pitted each of us against ourselves, each other, and the sea. We were injured, but not broken. We won.

13

After Words

Fourteen years later – much has changed.

Vivid, hard memories of the race experience haunted me for a year, in part due to long term consequences of MRSA, a terrible infection caused by the staph bacteria that took advantage of our many open wounds and devastated some of the crew. Ah, the crew. My feelings about them now are only slightly less complicated than they were fourteen years ago on the raging seas.

So how did the voyage change me? I am still and will forever battle self-esteem issues, but those many, many hours of contemplation opened a lot of doors. In the face of more physical and emotional anguish than I'd ever known before, I learned how to more easily quash – or at least recognize – those feelings of self-doubt, of guilt and recrimination. I have become more independent, doing as I believe. I have learned greater acceptance of myself and others. With that comes an increased appreciation of anger and its impact on others. Understanding that has regulated my hyper-sensitivity. As my son used to say as a toddler," you're not the boss of the universe." I guess I've figured out it is *not always about me.*

I have moved away from Boulder and my beloved Boulder Community Rowing and many dear friends, and was grand-parented into moving to Gloucester, Massachusetts. Here, I have had the privilege of rowing competitively and recreation-ally with Gloucester Gig Rowers, a fine group of smart, com-petitive, and warm people, just like rowers everywhere.

My teams here participate in all kinds of events, from all kinds of smaller local competitions to much larger scale rac-es including the Blackburn Challenge, a 26-mile ocean row around Cape Ann, the World Pilot Gig Championships on the Islands of Scilly in the UK, a 10-day wilderness row in British Columbia, and The Great River Race on the Thames. I also belong to the local dory rowing club and own an ocean rowing single. I row or cox an hour or two every day. Can I say that rowing is the backbone of my life?

Recently, I have been practicing with London Calling, a double ocean rowing boat leaving from Boston in 2026 to row the Atlantic via the northern route from Boston to London, a dangerous trip never yet completed successfully. Perhaps jok-ingly, they invited me to join the 4-man crew. Considering it, I passed the idea by my old ocean rowing buddy, Roger. He im-mediately and vigorously quashed it as too harrowing. There are reasons, he reminded me, why the goal has never been achieved. And, much as I hate to admit it, the Oldest Woman to Row the Atlantic is even older now.

My ongoing friendship with Roger has been both lovely and fruitful. Thanks to him, I have rowed in the flotilla of the Queen's Diamond Jubilee on the Thames for the 1000 boat salute as well as a few wonderful re-enactments: the Signing of the Magna Carta, the Battle of Waterloo, and the Boston Tea Party.

What about the rest of the crew? Despite the MRSA, each has forged ahead to live their best lives. I was delighted to try to contact each of them as a way of wrapping up the story.

It was such a pleasure to catch up with **Ben.** "After the row," he writes, "I found it hard to return to corporate life and started building businesses instead. It's a bit like rowing an ocean, you've just got to be mad enough to start." He tells me he is feeling fortunate to be able to play a key role in some major ecommerce successes and is currently building a new property project. No surprise there, brilliant as he is. He got married and lives in Southwest London with three cats, near the boathouse where the oars on *Britannia III* came from. "I'm mainly found on my bike these days," he says, "and supporting others attempting big endurance challenges."

Anna soared, as she has always done. She has traveled quite a bit and is married. Now an academic in Boston studying bioethics, she has two children. It was exciting to discover that she lives so close to Gloucester that we might be able to get together soon.

Mike, my gnarly fireman, wrote a book called *Three Dads Walking.* After the loss of his daughter, he currently campaigns and raises money for Papyrus Prevention of Young Suicide. According to Guy, Mike "has been instrumental in changing the law about suicide prevention in schools. He's helped so many people."

Shaun is fulfilling his dreams. He owns Our Joe Fishing Charters, spending his days fishing for blue marlin off the south coast of England. He is also an avid gig rower for Dart Gig Club.

Colin and I have exchanged birthday greetings over the years but little more. He married his long-time sweetheart, Sally, and they live in London. Amiable Colin has always been in the hospitality business and is currently the managing director of Lavender Green Flowers, London's *finest* florist.

Guy became a digital creator, living in Cardiff now, but possibly moving to Croatia. In our brief exchange, he spoke fondly of his wife and daughter. His warmth and kindness are still legend.

Our skipper, **Simon**, is famous in the world of ocean rowing. At this point, he has built more ocean rowing boats than anyone else, and has inspired and enabled hundreds of individuals to row an ocean (or two). He personally has rowed the Atlantic seven times and the Indian Ocean twice. Simon Chalk is in the Guinness World Records for "the most rows by one person" and is arguably the world's most experienced rower. Currently working at Cerberus Energy, he is married and has three children.

My dear buddy, **Roger**, owns a boatyard, Coates Marine, in Whitby, North Yorkshire, England. His son, Ben, runs the boatyard. Roger himself is involved in the upkeep and use of a former 1902 rowing lifeboat, the *William Riley* (www.official-williamriley.org.uk). "The rest of the family are doing well," he writes. "Recently our youngest daughter, Nicola, arranged the security for JD Vance's visit to the UK (like father, like daughter)." Roger has four terrific children and three grandchildren and a lovely wife who puts up with all of his shenanigans.

After the row, **Beth** "turned her passions to sailing." She holds a Coast Guard Merchant Mariner Credential (captain's license) and owns a Cape Dory 25. Professionally, she returned to teaching at the university level and then back into marketing communications in the institutional investment management industry. She tells me that the row didn't change her, a concept she explores in her first completed manuscript, *Rowing Nowhere,* and proves in her 2020 attempt to sail around the world after another period of loss, which is the subject of her second manuscript.

I could only catch up with **Nabs, Jonathan,** and **Jen** through their Facebook pages. Looks like Nabs is the chairman at Oman Rugby and (as always) a great adventurer. Jonathan appears to be married, living in New England and owner/president of a contracting firm.

According to her social media presence, MRSA may have hit Jenn worst of all. After sustaining a hairline fracture to her femur, she was admitted to St. Paul's Hospital. Within twenty-four hours she had developed progressive multi-organ failure, due to severe sepsis, possibly a result of the MRSA she contracted on our trip. She spent five months in the hospital. Still, a testament to her resilience, she continues to row in the Pacific Northwest.

Dan was, as ever, elusive, not to be found on the usual sources. Dan, I wish you well and thank you for the spork.

In a lifetime of adventures, I had the ultimate adventure, the supreme experience of my life. What a privilege.

Coda

April 4, 2011

Friends:

Our buddy is on land. Wobbly, but walking. The adventure was completed by the crew being detained by the customs officials at the port, angry because they had come in at night and had not stayed to clear customs. Well, OK, they were told they couldn't leave the Yacht Club until they were cleared.

Suzanne absolutely blew us away when she got off the boat. Beautiful, looking and talking like she had just finished a hike with the dogs. She's in phenomenal condition, physically (well, a few boils, a lot of aches, tendonitis) and mentally.

I talked to Simon, the Captain and asked if she had pulled her weight. He said yes, and then some. He said she was the rock of the crew. Never missed a shift rowing (the only crew member to do so). Rowed hard every minute. Never late. Never complained, never whined. Did whatever was asked of her and more. Supported all the crew members, consoled when needed, cajoled when needed, tended to their wounds, kept them all sane.

I wish I had a recording of my conversation with Colin, which made me cry when I read it. His message and a similar message from one of the women were written on the wall of the tiny compartment in which Suzanne slept, in a fetal position, with two men on their rest periods. Colin gave me about a five minute monologue about her exploits. Being an old guy, I can't really remember the anecdotes. But much in the vein of Simon's comments, he said the crew were in awe of her stability and commitment and felt that they owed what sanity they have left to her.

So we are enormously proud of her achievement in becoming the oldest and most beautiful woman to ever row across an ocean, but even prouder of the way she did it. With typical grace and style, passion and dogged determination. And 4 puppies and I are very happy to have her safely back.

Mike Enwall
Liberia Country Representative
International Legal Assistance Consortium (ILAC)
0613 6218

Acknowledgements

I would like to express my warm thanks to Maile Black and Winter Island Press, the editor, promoter, mentor and publish-er. Maile, you have been the greatest inspiration and believer in this book. Your insight, patience, and encouragement shaped this story into what it is.

Thanks, too, to the dear *Shut Up and Write* writers who are kind and talented and a great support. You all awe me.

I am indebted to my wonderful adventure-advocating family, my companions on too many experiences and adventures to keep straight. Thank you for your faith in me and for greeting us in Barbados!!! You are my light in the distance to strive toward.

To my Boulder Community Rowing friends who shaped me into a rower with love and support, and to my YMCA buddies who pushed hard workouts during the winter and were strong encouragers of this journey. And for Jennifer's inspiring words, "You are where you are supposed to be…"

I must wholeheartedly thank the courageous crew of *Brittania III*, especially Roger. This story includes you – all forty-two days. I hold you all in my heart,

Thank you to Gloucester Gig Rowers, my new rowing home. Your great encouragement, warm inclusion into your lives, and new rowing adventures make every day the best day.

Thank you to every reader who picks up this book: your time and attention are gifts and the reason I write.

Remember: We make it work, we always do.